# GLEANINGS FROM THE BOOK OF RUTH

# GLEANINGS
## FROM THE
# BOOK OF
# RUTH

ALEX DRYBURGH

GLEANINGS FROM THE BOOK OF RUTH
By: Alex Dryburgh
Copyright © 2014
GOSPEL FOLIO PRESS
All Rights Reserved

Published by
GOSPEL FOLIO PRESS
304 Killaly St. W.
Port Colborne, ON L3K 6A6
CANADA

ISBN: 9781927521618

Cover design by Danielle Elzinga
Photo by Amalrik Dumas

All Scripture quotations from the
King James Version unless otherwise noted.

Printed in USA

# ACKNOWLEDGEMENTS

There are several people I wish to thank who have been a huge help during this project.

First of all, I would like to thank my wife, Irene, for her lifelong support in the work of the Lord. She has provided much love and encouragement during the past four years it has taken to finalize this book.

Furthermore, I would like to express my deep gratitude to our brother in the Lord, John Fairfield. Without the work of our brother, this book would not have been possible. John has laboured countless hours editing my work and compiling my lifelong notes on the book of Ruth in a structured manner that we trust will bring the greatest blessing and benefit to the saints that pick up this book. I would like to thank John for his patience with me in this project. There were times when I was ready to call it quits but John was always there to pick me up and prod me along. I trust that our joint efforts on this undertaking will be a blessing to you all.

# PREFACE

This is not a commentary on the book of Ruth in the traditional sense. Many such good ones may be found elsewhere.

Rather it is summary of a lifetime of work studying this part of the Scriptures. Thus this book is more correctly a "gleanings" than a "commentary". This is a collection of gems accumulated over the years, rather than a systematic, analytical or expository work on the book of Ruth. An explanation of the term "gleanings", as used in this book, is laid out below.

Two main objectives are before us:

Firstly, that believers enjoy the gems relating to this lovely book as they are presented, just as one would enjoy daily manna —one small portion at a time. The reader may open this book to any page and enjoy the thoughts just as they are.

Secondly, we trust that this material, which is presented without embellishments, will be available for others beyond the writer's sphere of public ministry to develop and use in feeding the people of God. In other words, the aim is to provide the "bare bones" so others, including Sunday School teachers, may "flesh out" the material according to their needs and exercise. To that end, most Scripture quotations are referenced.

We begin with thoughts drawn from an overview of the entire book of Ruth, and then go on to consider lessons from each of its chapters. While the overview brings together fragments drawn from the book as a whole, the sections relating to the four chapters present a variety of thoughts and teachings drawn from the text. Each of these chapter related sections begins with comments drawn from the story as it unfolds, followed by teachings of a more practical nature. For convenience, each of these latter practical teachings are organized around four main headings. In addition, in chapters one and two, where gleanings about

"Backsliding and Recovery" and "The Field of Boaz" are given in considerable detail, these are presented as specific "highlights".

As an appendix, the topic of the "Untils" in the book of Ruth is further developed which generates more gleanings.

Frequently, the context is taken beyond the immediate scope of the book of Ruth, as examples from that book trigger a series of links to other parts of the Scriptures that are helpful and relevant to believers today. As a result of these objectives there is some overlap. To keep certain groups of gems in a sequential order it is necessary, at times, to repeat what may have been presented already. No apology is made for this.

## Gleanings

Gleaning is the act of collecting left over crops from a farmer's field. It is a very old practice, and is an early form of welfare. It involves gathering slowly and laboriously, bit by bit, and usually in fields.

Gleaning was practiced in Israel in Bible times as a means of providing relief for the poor and for strangers. The corners of fields were not to be reaped and the sheaves accidentally left behind in the fields, were to remain there, according to the Law of Moses (Lev. 19:9; 23:22; and Deut. 24:21). These were for the poor to glean. Similar laws applied to vineyards and olive yards. (Compare Ruth 2:2).

However, gleaning was back-breaking work, no easy task—nor was it swift.

The word "gleaning" may be applied in a figurative sense, as it is here. While literal "gleaning" is the stripping of a field of what is left by reapers, the term may be applied to the collecting, or gathering of other things, little by little, or slowly and in small pieces. Thus applied, the term means to learn, to discover, or to find out, and usually over time and in small amounts—just like the literal gleaning of crops in agriculture.

That is the picture that applies to the word "gleaning" as used in this volume, where it pertains to the accumulation of gems from the Scriptures, gathered slowly and laboriously and

## Preface

bit by bit, over a lifetime. Here the writer presents the results of gleanings from the Word of God, namely the presentation of gems acquired slowly, little by little and in small pieces.

In that sense, therefore, this book is about jewels to enrich the lives of those who love the Lord, rather than a systematic, academic analysis, profitable though the latter may be.

J. E. F.

# CONTENTS

An Introduction ........................................................... 13
Gleanings from the Whole Book of Ruth ............................ 15
*Chapter One*
    Ruth Cleaving to Naomi ............................................ 29
*Chapter Two*
    Ruth Gleaning in the Field ......................................... 49
*Chapter Three*
    Ruth Lying at The Feet .............................................. 65
*Chapter Four*
    Ruth Fruitful in Marriage .......................................... 83
The "Untils" of the Book of Ruth ....................................... 95

# AN INTRODUCTION

The book of Ruth has been likened to a sunny green valley between two mountain peaks of ice and snow. On the one side we have the book of Judges and on the other the first book of Samuel. The book of Judges presents a bleak picture. Four times in it we read that there was *"No king in Israel"*, and twice we read that everyone did *"that which was right in their own eyes"*. On the other hand, 1 Samuel isn't much better. That book begins with the blindness of Eli the high priest and the sin of the young men, his sons. We are told that in those days the word of the Lord was *"rare"* (1 Sam. 3:1), the lamp of God was going out, and there was no open vision. Even the story of the boy Samuel starts with godly Hannah being provoked by Peninnah.

But in between these two depressing books of carnality we have this delightful book of Ruth, with its heart warming story of recovery and devotion—all because of the grace of God. We should never judge a book on the basis of its size, but rather on its substance. Having only eighty-five verses in four chapters (fewer verses than in Psalm 119) the book of Ruth may be read in only twenty minutes. It may be very small in size, but it is large in substance.

Throughout this lovely book we see lines of truth that have relevance in the church age: principles, features and examples that should mark believers and influence their walk with God. For example, a consideration of the main personalities in the book (as we shall see in due course) proffers New Testament applications. In Boaz we see the truth of a **redeemer**, in Elimelech the thought of a **brother**, in Ruth the truth of a **builder**, in Naomi the truth of a **nurse**, and in Obed the thought of **progress**. This pattern is typical of many such examples and illustrations that shine on the pages of these lovely Scriptures.

# GLEANINGS FROM THE BOOK OF RUTH

The title of this book comes from the activity of Ruth when she came to Bethlehem at the beginning of the barley harvest. Indeed, for many of us, the mention of the word *"gleaning"* in connection with the Scriptures brings to mind the book of Ruth. The principle of gleaning may be linked in a progressive sequence of "days" of Scripture, which associate salvation with service, devotion, and enjoyment of the Word. Namely:

> The **day of salvation**: *"This day is salvation come to this house"* (Luke 19:9).
>
> The **day of occupation:** *"Go work to day in my vineyard"* (Matt. 21:28).
>
> The **day of consecration:** *"Who then is willing to consecrate his service this day?"* (1 Chron. 29:5).
>
> The **day of gleaning:** *"Where hast thou gleaned to day?"* (2:19).

This small book, being large of substance, offers much from which to glean.

# GLEANINGS FROM THE WHOLE BOOK OF RUTH

There are pictures and teachings to be derived from each respective chapter of the book of Ruth, but there is also much to be gained by considering all four chapters simultaneously, which we do here. Thoughts from this overview of the entire book are presented in three parts:

Gleanings from a general overview.
Gleanings regarding Ruth's person.
Gleanings regarding other characters in the book.

### Gleanings from an Overview of the Book of Ruth

The book of Ruth can be summarized as, "Ten years in Moab, a day in the field, a night at the feet and an hour at the gate," these relating to the book's four consecutive chapters.

**Chapter 1** tells of the **ten lost years in Moab**, and the workings of God in grace and government.

**Chapter 2** tells of the **day in the field of Boaz**, where Ruth is gleaning, gathering and giving.

**Chapter 3** tells of the **night at the feet of Boaz**, where Ruth gets more while resting at his feet than she does by working all day in his field.

**Chapter 4** tells of the **hour at the gate of the city of Bethlehem**, where Boaz presents the legal claims of Ruth.

The story of Ruth is truly uplifting—a contrast to many other books in the Bible, such as the Kings. Whereas in most books things go from bad to worse, in the book of Ruth things go from bad to good and then get even better! This can be highlighted with five illustrations.

> **Kingship:** The book begins with the thought of *"no king"* and ends with the genealogy of David, the *"great king"*.
>
> **Marriages:** The book begins with marriages that end in disaster and death, and ends with a marriage characterised by delight. The marriages in Moab (as well as that of Elimelech and Naomi) are neither fragrant nor fruitful, but the marriage of Boaz and Ruth is both fragrant and fruitful.
>
> **Inheritances:** The book begins with an inheritance lost, when Elimelech and Naomi left Bethlehem for Moab, and ends with the inheritance recovered after Naomi and Ruth come back.
>
> **Headship:** The book begins with headship lost, as seen in Elimelech, and ends with headship recovered, as seen in Boaz.
>
> **Sonship:** The book begins with sonship lost, as seen in Mahlon and Chilion, and ends with sonship restored, as seen in Obed.

It is not surprising, therefore, that in a book that is so uplifting there should be much about grace. In the four consecutive chapters, we see grace saving, serving, sanctifying and satisfying.

> **Chapter 1** illustrates **grace saving**, the truth of Ephesians 2:8-9: *"For by grace are ye saved through faith; and that not of yourselves…Not of works, lest any man should boast."*
>
> **Chapter 2** illustrates **grace serving**, the truth of Hebrews 12:28: *"Let us have grace, whereby we may serve God acceptably with reverence and godly fear."*
>
> **Chapter 3** illustrates **grace sanctifying**, the truth of Titus 2:12: *"Teaching us that, denying ungodliness and worldly lusts, we should live soberly, righteously, and godly, in this present world."*

## Gleanings from the Whole Book of Ruth

**Chapter 4** illustrates **grace satisfying,** the truth of 2 Corinthians 12:9: *"My grace is sufficient for thee: for my strength is made perfect in weakness."* The word *sufficient* carries with it the thought of contentment—of being satisfied.

Ruth herself makes reference to grace in this regard, when she says, *"Why have I found grace in thine eyes, that thou shouldest take knowledge of me, seeing I am a stranger?"* (2:10). The truth is that God's kindness is all you need.

In keeping with such examples of the grace of God, it can be seen that thoughts of commendation and care are not far from the surface in the book of Ruth.

**Commendation:** The recipient of this blessing is Ruth. She is commended by Naomi her mother-in-law, by the servants of Boaz who were in the field with her, by Boaz the redeemer, and by the women of the city. These all speak well of her.

**Care:** The thought of care permeates this little book, as typified in the relationship between Ruth and Naomi. It is very evident that Ruth cares for her mother-in-law, for she shows her kindness and gives her that which she has left after she is sufficed. Naomi responds by saying, *"the Lord deal kindly with you, as ye have dealt with the dead, and with me"* (1:8). Boaz finds out all this and gets a positive report from his servants in the field and says, *"It hath fully been shewed me, all that thou hast done unto thy mother in law"* (2:11).

A variety of important doctrinal and practical truths are pictured throughout the book of Ruth, and a systematic look at the four consecutive chapters reveals many of these. The following are offered as suggestions for personal consideration:

In chapter 1 there is the thought of **salvation.**

In chapter 2 there is the thought of **separation.**

In chapter 3 there is the thought of **sanctification.**

In chapter 4 there is the thought of **satisfaction.**

# GLEANINGS FROM THE BOOK OF RUTH

In chapter 1 we see **weeping**, when three women became widows.

In chapter 2 we see **working**, when Ruth worked with her hands in the field.

In chapter 3 we see **winnowing**, when Boaz spent the night on the threshing floor.

In chapter 4 we see **a wedding**, when Boaz took Ruth as his bride.

In chapter 1 Ruth is in **the country**—a widow marked by sorrow.

In chapter 2 Ruth is in **the field**—a gleaner.

In chapter 3 Ruth is in **the threshing floor**—a daughter and a virtuous woman.

In chapter 4 Ruth is in **her house**—a wife and a mother.

In chapter 1 we see Ruth as a **sinner who is saved**.

In chapter 2 we see Ruth as a **servant employed**.

In chapter 3 we see Ruth as a **priest in communion**.

In chapter 4 we see Ruth as a **bride who is married**.

(For this latter sequence I am indebted to the late John Douglas, of Ashgill, Scotland.)

## Gleanings Regarding Ruth's Person

All four chapters of the book display characteristics of the person and personality of Ruth, and from these lessons can be learned and pictures drawn. Some distinctions of Ruth that stand out are the **Role of God in her life**, her **Faith**, her **Beauty**, her **Character**, her **Walk** and her **Opinion of Herself**. Finally, as a complement to these, we consider what **Others say about her**.

### God in the Life of Ruth

It is important to see God in the life of Ruth throughout the book. A progression is suggested as the story unfolds, beginning with a simple blessing and concluding with a great blessing.

In chapter 1 Naomi says of her daughters-in-law, *"The Lord deal kindly with you, as ye have dealt with the dead, and with me"* (v. 8).

In chapter 2 Boaz says to Ruth, *"The Lord recompense thy work, and a full reward be given thee of the Lord God of Israel, under whose wings thou art come to trust"* (v. 12).

In chapter 3 Boaz says, *"Blessed be thou of the Lord, my daughter"* (v. 10).

In chapter 4 the elders of the city of Bethlehem say to Boaz, *"The Lord make the woman that is come into thine house like Rachel and like Leah"* (v. 11).

## Ruth and Faith

In her devotion to Naomi, to God and to the inheritance of God's people, Ruth displays a remarkable faith, as illustrated in a progression in the four chapters of the book.

**Faith's choice.** In the first chapter Ruth comes to a place where two ways meet and has to make a choice. On the one hand there is Moab with its carnal people and its defiling gods, and on the other hand is Bethlehem of Judea with its people and its God. Ruth makes the right choice, *"Thy people shall be my people, and thy God my God"* (v. 16).

**Faith's comfort.** In the second chapter Ruth says, *"Thou hast comforted me, and for that thou hast spoken friendly unto thine handmaid"* (v. 13). Faith and comfort link us to God, who is *"the God of all comfort"* (2 Cor. 1:3). Likewise there is comfort in Christ (Phil. 2:1) and the Holy Spirit is referred to as the Comforter (John 14:16). Ruth's comfort is because of the faith that had brought her this far.

**Faith's courage.** In the third chapter Ruth displays considerable bravery. For a young woman at night to go to a threshing floor would involve courage, especially in a strange culture.

> **Faith's compensation.** By the fourth chapter, however, the rewards of being in the mind of God become evident. The desolate widow of chapter one becomes a wife and a mother in chapter four.

## Ruth's Beauty

Ruth is such a lovely character that it is always assumed she is also a beautiful woman, and so she is. She has many beautiful features, but hers is the beauty that springs from within and lasts forever—it is much deeper than the skin. In the Scriptures there is a beauty that is vain as well as that which is virtuous. *"Favour is deceitful, and beauty is vain: but a woman that feareth the Lord, she shall be praised"* (Prov. 31:30).

Someone has said that one looking for a wife should look for four things; face, figure, faith and fidelity. While one may not get the first two, they should make sure they get the last two. We can't be sure if Ruth had the first two—but the picture painted by the Word shows that she certainly had the last two.

There are other beautiful things in the Scriptures too. We read of a beautiful face, of beautiful feet and of a beautiful flock.

> **The beautiful face** belongs to Abigail, who was a woman of good understanding as well as of a beautiful countenance.
>
> **The beautiful feet** are the feet of the Lord Jesus. His feet never strayed, slipped nor stumbled. He walked a perfect path of purest grace, unblemished and complete, for He was the spotless Nazarite, being pure—even to His feet.
>
> **The beautiful flock** is the assembly. Its beauty is seen as it is being fed, watered, and guarded.

## Ruth's Character

In general, it is can be seen that Ruth is a woman of a steadfast mind, a tender spirit, a loving heart, a subjective submissive will, willing and working hands, a holy character and a surrendered life.

## Gleanings from the Whole Book of Ruth

Something of Ruth's character is revealed in the four consecutive chapters of the book.

**Ruth's determination** in chapter 1: When Naomi sees that Ruth is steadfastly minded, she leaves off speaking to her. Not all determination is good, of course, and we are reminded that there is a determination that is not of God. Barnabas was determined to take with him John Mark whereas Paul, having the mind of God, thought it not good (Acts 15:37).

**Ruth's diligence** in chapter 2: She shows this in gleaning, gathering and giving.

**Ruth's dedication** in chapter 3: *"I am Ruth thine handmaid"* (v. 9). This is an act of devotion to the things of God.

**Ruth's devotion** in chapter 4: The women of Bethlehem tell Naomi that Ruth is *"thy daughter in law, which loveth thee"* (v. 15).

In the early stages of the story Ruth's character is manifested by what she does for others. In later stages, her character is testified by the actions of others doing things for her.

In the **first chapter** the salient comment of Naomi's that defines Ruth's character is, *"The Lord deal kindly with you, as ye have dealt with the dead, and with me"* (v. 8).

In the **second chapter** Boaz's observation is an evaluation of Ruth's behaviour, *"It hath fully been shewed me, all that thou hast done unto thy mother in law since the death of thine husband"* (v. 11).

However,

In the **third chapter** Naomi takes the initiative to provide for Ruth. She says, *"Shall I not seek rest for thee, that it may be well with thee"* (v. 1). Likewise, Boaz says to her, *"I will do to thee all that thou requirest"* (v. 11) and Naomi observes, *"The man will not be in rest, until he have finished the thing this day,"* (v. 18). Significantly, Boaz measures her six measures of barley.

# GLEANINGS FROM THE BOOK OF RUTH

In the **fourth chapter** Boaz purchases Ruth to be his wife.

Ruth's character parallels that of the believer in the Age of Grace, and her faith and behaviour are an example to all in this present age. In that regard, she is a woman who has on the breastplate of faith, the girdle of humility, the robe of righteousness, the garment of holiness and the great overcoat of love. These garments should be worn by every Christian today.

> **The breastplate and the helmet**: *"But let us, who are of the day, be sober, putting on the breastplate of faith and love; and for an helmet, the hope of salvation"* (1 Thess. 5:8).
>
> **The girdle of humility**: *"Be clothed with humility"* (1 Pet. 5:5). Gird yourself with humility, and serve one another.
>
> **The robe of righteousness**: We have to be righteous, even as He is righteous, and follow after righteousness. *"We should live soberly, righteously, and godly, in this present world"* (Tit. 2:12). It is good to remember that *"soberly"* is **selfward**, *"righteously"* is **manward**, and *"godly"* is **Godward**.
>
> **The garment of holiness**: Like as He who has called you is holy. Be ye holy in all manner of living in every department of your life. Put on therefore as the elect of God, holy and beloved (1 Pet. 1:15).
>
> **The great overcoat of love**: *"Above all these things put on love, which is the bond of perfectness"* (Col. 3:14).

## Ruth's Walk

In as much as one's walk is determined by one's character, so a consideration of the latter leads to a description of the former. In Ruth's case it is apparent that she is a woman who moves in a path that is contrary to nature.

> **In chapter 1.** She is prepared to leave her people and her people's gods for Bethlehem of Judea. She is prepared to follow her mother-in-law.
>
> **In chapter 2.** She is coming after him in whose sight she would find grace. She finds favour with Boaz and says,

## Gleanings from the Whole Book of Ruth

"*Why have I found grace in thine eyes, that thou shouldest take knowledge of me, seeing I am a stranger?*" (v. 10). Also, she comes behind the reapers.

**In chapter 3.** She spends one night at the feet of Boaz—an act of faith in a strange culture.

**In chapter 4.** She is joined to Boaz in marriage, not to one of the young men, which would have been quite natural.

Ruth's walk shows a progression in the consecutive chapters of the book.

In chapter 1, Ruth is **strengthening herself.** "*She was steadfastly minded*" (v. 18).

In chapter 2, Ruth is **separating herself,** and she satisfies herself. "*And Boaz said unto her, At mealtime come thou hither, and eat of the bread, and dip thy morsel in the vinegar. And she sat beside the reapers: and he reached her parched corn, and she did eat, and was sufficed, and left*" (v. 14). Her separation, by going "*not to glean in another field*" (v. 8) brings her satisfaction.

In chapter 3, Ruth is **sanctifying herself.** "*Wash thyself therefore, and anoint thee, and put thy raiment upon thee*" (v. 3).

In chapter 4, Ruth is **subjecting herself.** The principle illustrated in chapter 4 is seen in the expression of verse 9 of chapter 3, when she says, "*I am Ruth thy handmaid.*" She is, in effect, saying, "You can have all you will of me."

## Ruth about Herself

It is typical of Ruth that she is modest, whereas others are more forthcoming about her virtues. An example of a believer who acknowledges the grace of God in life, Ruth says very little about herself. This is the truth of Proverbs 27:2, "*Let another man praise thee, and not thine own mouth; a stranger, and not thine own lips.*" When referring to herself she identifies with being a stranger and a slave.

In chapter 2 she speaks of herself as a **stranger**. She says, *"Why have I found grace in thine eyes, that thou shouldest thou take knowledge of me, seeing I am a stranger?"* (v. 10).

In chapter 3 she speaks of herself as a **slave**. She says, *"I am Ruth thy handmaid"* — a female slave (v. 9).

## Others about Ruth

Others, on the other hand, are more flattering about Ruth than she is about herself.

> **Naomi** speaks about her **kindness.** *"The Lord deal kindly with you, as ye have dealt with the dead, and with me"* (1:8).
>
> **The servant set over the reapers** speaks of her being **Consistent.** *"[She] hath continued even from the morning until now, that she tarried a little in the house"* (2:7).
>
> **Boaz** speaks about her **faith**. *"It hath fully been shewed me, all that thou hast done unto thy mother in law since the death of thy husband: and how thou hast left thy father and thy mother, and the land of thy nativity, and art come unto a people which thou knewest not heretofore"* (2:11).
>
> **Boaz** speaks of her **virtue**. *"All the city ..... doth know that thou art a virtuous woman"* (3:11).
>
> **The women of the city** speak of her **love**. *"Thy daughter in law, which loveth thee, which is better to thee than seven sons, hath born him"* (4:15).

## Gleanings Regarding Others in the Book of Ruth

The various individuals who are part of the story of Ruth are, in themselves, of interest. Firstly, the mere list of those in this "cast" tells a story just by itself. Secondly, there is much to be learned from those who are the direct objects of blessing from the Lord. Finally, the developing relationship between Ruth and Boaz illustrates the relationship between the believer and Christ.

# Gleanings from the Whole Book of Ruth

## The "Cast"

There are nine main characters mentioned in the book of Ruth, not counting those listed in the genealogy at the end. Seven of those characters are named and two are unnamed. This, of itself, is significant.

**The seven who are named:** Elimelech (My God is King), Naomi (Pleasant, Agreeable), Mahlon (Sickness), Chilion (Pining), Ruth (Beauty, or Satisfied), Boaz (In him is strength) and Orpah (Neck, or Skull). Of these, the three main characters in the book are Boaz, Naomi and Ruth.

However, not all persons necessarily live up to the promise of their names.

> **Ruth** lived true to her name ("Beauty" or "Satisfied").
>
> **Elimelech** belied his name ("My God is King").
>
> **Naomi** changed her name."*Call me not Naomi* ("Pleasant"), *call me Mara* ("Bitter") (1:20).

In this story,

> **Ruth is the privileged person.** She says, *"Why have I found grace in thine eyes?"* and asks Boaz why he would *"take knowledge of me, seeing I am a stranger?"* (2:10)
>
> **Boaz is the preeminent person.** Boaz is the mighty man of wealth and a mighty man of valour. He is lord and master of the field. More importantly, he is the kinsman redeemer.
>
> **Naomi is a prominent person.** Although seemingly a lesser character, she is mentioned in every chapter.

In addition there is **Obed**, the son to Boaz and Ruth, whose name means "Serving". Although passive in this story, Obed's name is important in the genealogy of David. He is famous in Israel and is a restorer and a nourisher to Naomi and to the entire family line. The inheritance is restored to him and he becomes the father of Jesse and the grandfather of David, and is part of the restoration of Israel. His name is a reminder we have been saved to serve.

# GLEANINGS FROM THE BOOK OF RUTH

**The two who are not named:** The **servant set over the reapers** and the **kinsman nearer than Boaz**. The servant set over the reapers is a type of the Spirit of God who does not speak of Himself, and the nearer kinsmen is a type of the law. In the latter case, he is not named because of his weakness. While the law is perfect it needs perfect material to work with. In the nearer kinsman we see the law being weak through the flesh and thus he is an illustration of the law not being able to do what Christ could.

## Those Blest of the Lord

Boaz, Ruth and Naomi are recorded as having been blest of the Lord.

> **Naomi says it about Boaz.** *"Blessed be he of the Lord, who hath not left off his kindness to the living and to the dead"* (2:20).
>
> Boaz is blest of the Lord because of the kindness he showed to the living and to the dead. He showed kindness, not only to Naomi and Ruth, but to the memory of Elimelech, Mahlon and Chilion. Boaz is blest of the Lord because of his interest in Ruth and the kindness he had shown her (2:20).
>
> **Boaz says it about Ruth.** *"Blessed be thou of the Lord my daughter: for thou has shewed more kindness in the latter end than at the beginning, inasmuch as thou followedst not young men, whether poor or rich"* (3:10).
>
> Ruth is blest of the Lord because of the kindness she had shown.
>
> *"The Lord recompense thy work, and a full reward be given thee of the Lord God of Israel"* (2:12).
>
> *"The Lord deal kindly with you, as ye have dealt with the dead, and with me"* (1:8).
>
> *"It hath fully been shewed me, all that thou has done unto thy mother in law since the death of thine husband"* (2:11).
>
> **The women of the city say it about Naomi.** *"Blessed be the Lord, which hath not left thee this day without a kinsman"* (4:14).

Naomi is blest of the Lord because of the kindness she had shown. In fact, in the person of Naomi we see a number of lovely truths:

The truth of the **Evangelist** in chapter 1.
The truth of the **Teacher** in chapters 2 and 3.
The truth of the **Pastor** in chapter 4.

(For this I am indebted to the late John Douglas, of Ashgill, Scotland.)

## The Relationship of Ruth and Boaz

Finally, as the book of Ruth develops, there is a significant progression recorded in the way Ruth becomes more and more acquainted with Boaz. Such a relationship illustrates the bond between the believer in the Age of Grace and the Lord Himself.

> In chapter 1, **Ruth hears about Boaz** as Naomi speaks about her people and her God. Ruth's response is, *"Thy people shall be my people, and thy God my God"* (v. 16).
>
> In chapter 2, **Boaz hands Ruth some parched corn**. She is labouring in his field and sitting with his reapers at meal time when this takes place.
>
> In chapter 3, **Ruth spends a night at the feet of Boaz**. This is a place of **well-being**, a place of **enlightenment**, a place of **encouragement** and a place of **enrichment**.
>
> In chapter 4, **Ruth is joined to Boaz** in holy matrimony. He is the **source** of life, the **strength** of life, the **sustenance** of life and the **satisfaction** of life.

The illustration is simple. We, as the people of God, should become more and more intimate with our heavenly Boaz as we get to know Him as Saviour. Mary's statement, *"My soul doth magnify the Lord, and my spirit hath rejoiced in God my Saviour"* (Luke 1:46-47) should be ours. We should seek to know Him, not only as Saviour, but as Lord.

## Chapter One

# RUTH CLEAVING TO NAOMI

The first chapter of Ruth is dominated by tragedy and triumph. The tragedy is the move to Moab and the subsequent deaths of a husband (Elimelech) and two sons (Mahlon and Chilion). The further heartbreak of the departure of Orpah only adds to that tragedy. The triumph comes with the move to Bethlehem of Judea (v. 22), together with the restoration of Naomi and the continuation of Ruth.

There are lessons to be learned from the major teachings of this chapter, with special emphasis on backsliding and recovery, together with practical considerations that relate to our own age. Thus, for discussion purposes, this section is presented in three parts:

1. Gleanings from the chapter as a whole.
2. Highlight: Backsliding and Recovery.
3. Four Practical Thoughts about the Believer's Walk.

### Gleanings from Ruth Chapter One

We begin with some thoughts about **grace and government** because the grace of God is foremost in all of the book of Ruth, even when God deals in correction. This leads to the subject of **widows,** the result of mistaken **decisions.** While the grace of God is paramount, decisions we make have outcomes for which we are responsible, so the context of such decisions, whether they be made by the **spiritual**, the **natural** or the **carnal**, is relevant. In turn decisions lead to **turning points** in a believer's walk and, as in this case, can lead to a **walk out of God's will** that resulted in three destitute widows. Finally, because there is more than one aspect to a death, we consider the role of famine. Fortunately, although the poor decisions of Ruth chapter 1 bring grief, it is cheering to note that good decisions follow.

## Grace and Government

The grace of God and the government of God are seen in chapter 1. Grace is often associated with other truths.

> Sometimes we read about grace and glory. *"The Lord will give grace and glory: no good thing will he withhold from them that walketh uprightly"* (Ps. 84:11).
>
> Sometimes we read about grace and truth. *"The law was given by Moses, but grace and truth came by Jesus Christ"* (John 1:17).
>
> Sometimes we read about grace and peace. *"Grace be unto you, and peace, from God our Father"* (1 Cor. 1:3).

In this chapter we read about **grace and government**.

When Naomi speaks about others she speaks about the **goodness of God**.

> *"The Lord had visited his people in giving them bread"* (v. 6).
>
> *"The Lord deal kindly with you, as ye have dealt with the dead, and with me"* (v. 8).

But when Naomi speaks about herself she mentions the **government of God**.

> *"The hand of the Lord is gone out against me"* (v. 13).
>
> *"The Almighty hath dealt very bitterly with me"* (v. 20).
>
> *"I went out full, and the Lord hath brought me home again empty…The Lord hath testified against me"* (v. 21).

## Ruth Cleaving to Naomi

We ought to be slow to see the government of God in the lives of others, but be quick to see the government of God in our own life.

## Widows

The final stage of departure from the will of God in this chapter is tragedy that leaves three women in widowhood. Various types of widows are defined in the New Testament, and three of these are illustrated in the first chapter of Ruth; the "widow indeed", the "widow who gives herself to pleasure", and the "young widow who guides the home". Paul, writing 1 Timothy 5, identified four types of widows:

> **The widow indeed.** A woman who is totally desolate, with no means of support, but who trusts in God. She continues in supplication and prayers night and day. Paul taught that we are to show respect to such and *"Honour widows that are widows indeed"* (1 Tim. 5:3).
>
> However, Paul taught that the rich should have the same attitude of dependence on God. He himself referred to his trust in God, even when he worked to support himself. *"For therefore we both labour and suffer reproach, because we trust in the living God, who is the Saviour of all men, specially of those that believe"* (1 Tim. 4:10). The rich man, Paul said, should also trust in *"the living God, who giveth us richly all things to enjoy"* (1 Tim. 6:17). Paul knew poverty and Paul knew prosperity, but in both circumstances he trusted in the living God.
>
> The widow woman in her poverty, the "widow indeed", trusts in the living God and likewise, the rich man, in his prosperity, trusts in the living God.
>
> **The widow with family.** This is a widow with children and grandchildren.
>
> **The widow who gives herself to pleasure.** A widow who uses her lack of responsibilities to go in for pleasure, she is *"dead while she lives"*.

**The younger widow.** A widow who is young enough to provide for herself, she is to marry, bear children and guide a home.

Three of those widows are seen in the book of Ruth. In Naomi is the "widow indeed". She has neither children nor grandchildren, but trusts in the living God. Orpah is the widow who "gives herself to pleasure" and is "dead while she lives". Ruth, on the other hand, is the "younger widow" who marries, bears children and who guides the home.

## Decisions

In many ways Ruth chapter 1 is a chapter of decisions, both right and wrong. The tragedy and recovery described in the beginning of the story are the result of such decisions, both good and bad. Wrong decisions lead to widowhood, but right decisions lead to recovery.

In this chapter there are **wrong decisions**:

> **Elimelech** makes a wrong decision about the **dwelling place**. He decides to give up Bethlehem-Judah, the house of bread and the house of praise, for Moab, the "desirable" land.
>
> **Mahlon and Chilion** make wrong decisions about **marriage**. Mahlon decides to marry Ruth, a Moabitess, and **Chilion** decides to marry Orpah, a Moabitess, despite God's injunction about intermarriage with idolaters.
>
> **Orpah** makes a wrong decision about **worship**. She decides to return to her country and to her gods.

But in this chapter, there are also **right decisions**:

> Naomi decides **to return from** the land of Moab.
>
> Ruth decides **to go to** the land of Naomi's God.
>
> Together they decide **to return to** Bethlehem-Judah.

# Ruth Cleaving to Naomi

## Natural, Carnal and Spiritual

Decisions are made within the context of the spiritual condition of the characters in question, whether they are natural, carnal or spiritual. In the Scriptures we see the **natural man,** the **carnal man** and the **spiritual man.**

> The **natural man** is without Christ and resists the Spirit.
>
> The **carnal man** denies Christ and grieves the Spirit.
>
> The **spiritual man** magnifies Christ and is filled with the Spirit.
>
> **In the book of Genesis** we have all three; Terah, the natural man, Lot the carnal man and Abraham the spiritual man.
>
> **In the Acts of the apostles** we have all three; Ananias, the high priest, is the natural man (ch. 23). Ananias (and Sapphira) is the carnal man (ch. 5). Ananias the disciple is the spiritual man, and a devout man (ch. 9).
>
> **In the first chapter of the book of Ruth** we have all three: Orpah is the natural, Elimelech is the carnal, and Naomi and Ruth are the spiritual ones, Ruth turning to God from idols.

## "Turning" in Scripture

Decisions determine one's walk and, in turn, lead to key turning points in life, for the connection between the two is close. This is illustrated in the book of Ruth, where the importance of various turning points in the lives of the principals is displayed. In the Scriptures, in general, there are turnings that are of God and turnings that are not of God.

In chapter 1 of the book of Ruth Elimelech and Orpah display turnings that are not of God, while Naomi and Ruth are examples of a turning that is of God.

> **Elimelech** turns from his inheritance in Bethlehem-Judah and goes down to Moab.
>
> **Orpah** leaves Naomi and Ruth and goes back to the idolatry of Moab.

**Naomi and Ruth**, on the other hand, turn their backs on sinful Moab and come to Bethlehem and the God of Israel.

## Turnings in Scripture That Are of God.

The Psalmist could say, *"Turn us again, O God, and cause thy face to shine; and we shall be saved"* (Ps. 80:3).

Paul noted the change in his converts in Thessalonica, specifically, *"how ye turned to God from idols to serve the living and true God; And to wait for his Son from heaven"* (1 Thess. 1:9-10).

The Psalmist reflected on the deliverance of his people by writing, *"When the Lord turned again the captivity of Zion, we were like them that dream"* (Ps. 126:1).

In those verses we have a turning that is of God.

> Out of my bondage, sorrow, and night,
> Jesus, I come! Jesus, I come!
> Into Thy freedom, gladness and light,
> Jesus, I come to Thee!
> Out of my sickness into Thy health,
> Out of my want and unto Thy wealth,
> Out of my sin and into Thyself,
> Jesus, I come to Thee!
>
> *Jesus, I Come*, William T. Sleeper

## Turnings in Scripture That Are Not of God.

There are those that have turned aside after Satan (1 Tim. 5:15).

All in Asia turned away from Paul, the apostle of God (2 Tim. 1:15).

Some turned aside unto vain talking (1 Tim. 1:6).

Paul told of the time coming when some would turn away their ears from the truth, and be turned unto fables (2 Tim. 4:4).

# Ruth Cleaving to Naomi

## Out of God's will

Poor decision making and poor turning points on the part of the key figures in the book of Ruth result in their being out of God's will. In the Scriptures, as a whole, there are various ways in which a believer can be out of God's will.

Sometimes it is **our own house instead of the house of God**. We see that in the book of Haggai, where the writer admonishes the people for living, *"in your cieled houses, and this house* (the house of God) *lie waste"* (Hag. 1:4).

> Sometimes it is our **own things and not the things that are of Christ Jesus**. *"For all seek their own, not the things which are Jesus Christ's"* (Phil. 2:21).
>
> Sometimes it is **our thoughts and our ways and not the thoughts of God or the ways of God**. *"For my thoughts are not your thoughts, neither are your ways my ways, saith the Lord"* (Isa. 55:8).
>
> Sometimes it is **our will and not the will of God**. *"Ye ought to say, If the Lord will, we shall live, and do this, or that"* (Jas. 4:15).

In chapter 1 of the book of Ruth, we see people doing their own will instead of the will of God.

> Elimelech **leaves his inheritance** and Bethlehem-Judah for Moab. It is his own will—not the will of God.
>
> Mahlon **marries** Ruth and Chilion marries Orpah, both Moabitesses. It is their own will—not the will of God.
>
> Orpah **returns** to her people and to her gods. It's her own will—not the will of God.

Elimelech's name means my "God is king" but God is not king in his life. Self is king in the life of Elimelech. We should not let sin rule as a monarch, or as a king, in our mortal body. In the garden of Gethsemane the Lord set the example for us when He said, *"Not my will but thine be done"* (Luke 22:42). We often say, "Not thy will but mine be done."

Elimelech is a man who has good intentions but he does not have the mind of God.

> In verse 1 he **sojourns** there.
>
> In verse 2 he **continues** there.
>
> In verse 4 he **dwells** there ten years.

The sojourner becomes the earth dweller. Let's make it very clear—**In the will of God there is no such thing as defeat, and outside the will of God there is no such thing as success.**

## Famines

Famine is the result of being out of God's will. It brings out what is real and what is false, and can be applied to both the physical and the spiritual. In the book of Ruth it is both, for the famine in the land brings out the famine in the soul.

There are two famines in Ruth chapter 1—a famine in the land of Moab, and a famine in Bethlehem-Judah. Of these two, the famine in Moab far exceeds the famine in Bethlehem-Judah. When Naomi leaves Bethlehem-Judah, she goes out full. When she returns, she comes back empty.

Many Scriptures display God's use of famine.

> **Famine of soul.** Amos reminds us of a famine of the soul. *"Behold, the days come, saith the Lord GOD, that I will send a famine in the land, not a famine of bread, nor a thirst for water, but of hearing the words of the LORD"* (Amos 8:11).
>
> **Famine of body.** It was a famine that brought the prodigal back to the father. He said, *"How many hired servants of my father's have bread enough and to spare, and I perish with hunger!"* (Luke 15:17).

## Highlight: Backsliding and Recovery

The story of the first chapter of Ruth is dominated by backsliding. It is a chapter of **disobedience, distress, disappointment, discouragement, defeat** and **death**.

## Ruth Cleaving to Naomi

Backsliding is against a **person** as seen in God.

Backsliding is against a **people** as seen in the people of God.

Backsliding is against a **place** as seen in the assembly.

Fortunately, the story in Ruth chapter 1 does not end there, for it goes on to recovery, and the main characters are illustrations of these steps.

In Elimelech we see the thought of **backsliding.**

In Naomi we see the thought of **recovery.**

In Ruth we see **spiritual growth.**

While **backsliding** and **recovery** are the main topics in this section, some thoughts about **safekeeping** from backsliding are likewise considered below.

## Backsliding

Backsliding is an important theme in Ruth chapter 1. In the chapter can be seen:

The **Cause** of backsliding.

The **Cost** of backsliding.

The **Cure** for backsliding.

(This is developed more fully later in this chapter, under "The Thought of Receiving").

The backslider in heart is one who is filled with **his own ways, and not God's.** Today, in the church age, a backslider is not a person who is away from the meeting; it is a person who is away from the Lord.

In the book of Jeremiah, Israel is portrayed as forsaking three things:

They forsake the **Lord.**

They forsake the **Law.**

They forsake the **Land.**

Backsliding is **a turning from God**, as can be seen in the life of Solomon. This great king's life can be divided into two:

> At first it was **beautiful with holiness**. Solomon loved the Lord and there was a day when the Lord was pleased with Solomon. It pleased the Lord that Solomon had asked for wisdom to rule His people, and he received it (1 Kgs. 3:10).
>
> Later it was **blasted with idolatry**. The Lord was angry with Solomon because his heart was turned away from the Lord. He loved many strange women (1 Kgs. 11:1, 9).

Backsliding is **leaving our first love.** It appeared early in the church age, and was a grief to Paul the Apostle. He noticed it at Corinth and in Galatia.

> The Corinthians departed from the simplicity that is in Christ (2 Cor. 11:3).
>
> The Galatians started well but their spiritual ardour cooled with time. Paul said to them that they did run well, and then asked, *"who did hinder you, or who did drive you back? Why did you turn back again unto the weak and beggarly elements?"* (Gal. 5:7, 4:9).

One of the great tragedies of backsliding is that, often, a person who backslides takes others with him.

> **Abraham** went down to Egypt and took Lot with him.
>
> **Jehoshaphat** went to Samaria and took others with him.
>
> **Peter** went fishing and took others with him. I believe that John chapter 21 is a scene of backsliding. The key words are night, naked, nets and nothing.
>
> **Elimelech** goes down to Moab, and takes others with him (ch. 1).

The **results of backsliding** among the people of God, as illustrated in Jeremiah 5:6, can be terrible. Jeremiah, in that context, likens it to attacks of the lion, the wolf and the leopard (or the panther).

## Ruth Cleaving to Naomi

> The **lion** slays.
>
> The **wolf** spoils.
>
> The **panther** slaughters and tears in pieces.

Why does Jeremiah relate this to Israel? Because their transgressions were many and their backslidings were increased.

**When a person leaves an assembly** that person does three things.

> Turns his back on a **place.**
>
> Turns his back on a **people.**
>
> Turns his back on a **person.**

The three types of people we saw earlier, spiritual, carnal and natural, can be seen in the assembly:

> **The spiritual man** we will call the heavy weight.
>
> **The carnal man** we will call the light weight.
>
> **The natural man** we will call the dead weight.

## Safekeeping

For our safekeeping and prevention from backsliding we should never lose sight of who God is, and of who you and I are. Elimelech's name is "My God is king", but he loses sight of this.

God is greatly **to be praised** for what He has done.

> *"Oh that men would praise the Lord for his goodness, and for his wonderful works to the children of men!"* (Ps. 107:8).

God is greatly **to be feared** for who He is.

> **God is the Father**—we are the children.
>
> **God is the Husbandman**—we are the branches.
>
> **God is the Shepherd**—we are the sheep.
>
> **God is the Potter**—we are the clay.

**God is the Master**—we are the servants.

**God is the King**—we are the subjects.

When you and I worship, we worship the King. In Malachi God is presented as a Father, as a Master and as a Great King. He says, *"If then I be a father, where is mine honour? And if I be a master, where is my fear?"* (Mal. 1:6). To this we should add, "If I be a great King where is my worship?" In Chronicles the potters dwelt with the king for his work (1 Chron. 4:23). Their service was communion with his work.

God's throne is a throne of grace.

> Thou art coming to a King;
> Large petitions with thee bring;
> For His grace and power is such,
> None can ever ask too much.

## Recovery

It is lovely that chapter 1 ends on an optimistic note, for backsliding gives way to recovery. In the person of Naomi there are a number of examples of recovery.

**Recovery to a place.** *"They went on the way to return unto the land of Judah"* (v. 7).

**Recovery to a people.** *"Surely we will return with thee unto thy people"* (v. 10).

**Recovery to a person.** Ruth says to Naomi, *"Thy God* (shall be) *my God"* (v. 16).

**Recovery to a home.** *"The Lord hath brought me home again empty"* (v. 21).

It is the thought of bread that brings Naomi from Moab to Bethlehem-Judah, just as it was the thought of bread that brought the prodigal from the far country to the father's house. When you get the thought of limitation it is never from the divine side but from the human side. The storehouses of the Lord are full, and there is bread enough and to spare.

## Ruth Cleaving to Naomi

Within our reach, and within our grasp, there are four things that are **unlimited.**

In spite of our ignorance there is **unlimited knowledge.**

In spite of our weakness there is **unlimited strength.**

In spite of our poverty there is **unlimited wealth.**

In spite of our leanness (of soul) there is **unlimited provision.**

**Unlimited knowledge** is within our grasp.

We bemoan the fact that ignorance is among us when unlimited knowledge is within our grasp. The Spirit guides us into all truth, and searches all things—the deep things of God. The river of God is full of water.

**Unlimited wealth** is within our grasp.

In Christ are hid all the treasures of wisdom and knowledge. We have been blessed with every spiritual blessing in the heavenly places in Christ Jesus. All things are yours, for you belong to Christ and Christ belongs to God.

**Unlimited strength** is within our reach.

Strength linked with **God** (Ps. 27).

Strength linked with **Christ** (Phil. 4).

Strength linked with **the Spirit of God** (Eph. 3).

Strength linked with **the grace of God** (2 Tim. 2).

**Unlimited provision** is ours.

The richness of God's inheritance is the attraction to Naomi. When she hears of the unlimited provision of God for His people, she wants to come back.

## Four Practical Thoughts About the Believer's Walk

In this chapter we can glean four practical thoughts from which we can learn lessons for ourselves.

# GLEANINGS FROM THE BOOK OF RUTH

**The thought of leaving:** Elimelech leaves Bethlehem for Moab, Orpah leaves Naomi and Ruth for Moab, and Naomi and Ruth leave Moab for Bethlehem-Judah.

**The thought of grieving:** The death of the husband and the death of two sons brings grief.

**The thought of cleaving:** Ruth cleaved to her mother in law.

**The thought of receiving:** All the city is moved when Naomi returns, and are shocked at her appearance. "Is this Naomi?" they say.

## The Thought Of Leaving

In Ruth chapter 1 Elimelech leaves Bethlehem Judah for Moab—he leaves the right place for the wrong place. Later, Naomi and Ruth leave Moab for Bethlehem-Judah—they leave the wrong place for the right place. Time and again in the Scriptures we see men in relation to places. Sometimes we see the right man in the right place, sometimes we see the wrong man in the right place, and sometimes we see the right man in the wrong place.

### *A Right Man in the Right Place*

**David** was such a man. *"One thing have I desired of the Lord"*, he said, *"that will I seek after; that I may dwell in the house of the Lord all the days of my life, to behold the beauty of the Lord, and to inquire in his temple"* (Psalm 27:4). Whether it be David in the palace, or David in the cave, or David in the House of God, he was the right man in the right place.

**Simeon** was the right man in the right place. He was a righteous devout man in Jerusalem, looking for the consolation of Israel, the Holy Spirit being upon him. He came in the Spirit into the temple, and blessed God, and he blessed the people of God. He was the right man in the right place.

# Ruth Cleaving to Naomi

**The Lord Jesus** was always the right man in the right place. Whether He was going up to Jerusalem, going through Samaria, or being in the midst of the two or three gathered together in His name, he was always saying the right things and doing the right things in the right way and the right manner.

## A Wrong Man in the Right Place

**Diotrephes**, in the third epistle of John, is a typical example of such a man. That man showed no signs of divine life and did three things:

> He displaced Christ (for he loved to have the pre-eminence, which is the right of Christ only).
>
> He kept out servants of God.
>
> He cast out saints of God.

## A Right Man in the Wrong Place

The **young man** in Judges 17 was a Levite who dwelled and functioned in the house of Micah. He was the right man—but he was in the wrong place.

> He gave up Bethlehem-Judah for the house of Micah in Ephraim.
>
> He gave up sojourning for dwelling.
>
> He gave up being a Levite to become a priest.
>
> He was content to dwell with the man in Ephraim because of three things:
>
>> Because of a **salary** (Ten pieces of silver by the year).
>>
>> Because of a **suit** (Garments to put on).
>>
>> Because of **sustenance** (Room and board).

Thus, we can see that **Elimelech** is the right man but he is in the wrong place. He leaves Bethlehem-Judah for Moab. He leaves Bethlehem-Judah, the house of bread and the house of praise, for Moab—a land that to him is desirable.

One thing to be sure of is this; a right man never makes a wrong place right and a wrong man never makes a right place wrong. We ought to be separate from the world in every shape and form.

> Separated from the **world of Egypt,** with its pleasure and its treasure.
>
> Separated from the **world of Sodom**, with its vice.
>
> Separated from the **world of Babylon**, with its music.
>
> Separated from the **world of Moab**, with its pride.

The call is always to come out from among them and be separate.

## The Thought of Grieving

Grieving is reflected in Naomi's comments about the goodness of God. When she speaks about the goodness of God she is thinking about others.

> While in the country of Moab, word reaches her of the goodness of God to His people in giving them bread.
>
> On the way back home, she trusts that the Lord will deal kindly with her daughters-in-law, as they had dealt with the dead and with her.

Grieving is brought about by **the government of God.** When speaking on the government of God, be slow to see it in the lives of others but be quick to see it in your own life. Naomi blames no one but herself, as she says;

> "*I went out full, and the Lord hath brought me home again empty*" (v.21).
>
> "*… it grieveth me much for your sakes that the hand of the Lord is gone out against me*" (v.13).
>
> "*The Almighty hath dealt very bitterly with me*" (v. 20).

She could summarize her sojourn in Moab;

## Ruth Cleaving to Naomi

> I went out a **wife**, I came back a **widow**.
>
> I went out a **mother** with two sons, and came back a mother, **motherless**.
>
> I went out **well known**, I came back **unknown**.
>
> I went out knowing the **grace of God**, I came back knowing the **government of God**.

The actions of God bring about grieving, and with it tears. There are two types of tears in the Bible: **tears of affliction and tears of affection**. Often where you find the one you find the other. In Ruth chapter one we see both:

> **Tears of affection** when Naomi kisses her daughters-in law and they lift up their voices and weep.
>
> **Tears of affliction** when the three husbands die – the death of Naomi's husband and the deaths of the two sons.

Tears of affliction and tears of affection are illustrated in the New Testament too. We see both at the death of Lazarus in John chapter 11.

> **Mary** shed tears of affliction because a brother had died.
>
> **The Jews**, in that place, shed tears of affection for they could see that Mary loved her brother.
>
> **The Lord Jesus**, wept tears of affection in Bethany.
>
> The Lord Jesus wept tears of **affection**.
>
> The Lord Jesus wept tears of **sympathy**.
>
> The Lord Jesus wept tears of **sorrow**.
>
> The Lord Jesus wept tears of **suffering**.

The same tears are reflected in Paul's teachings. When he had his last meeting with the elders of Ephesus, as recorded in Acts twenty, Paul told of his tears.

> **Tears of affliction**: Paul told them of his, *"Serving the Lord with all humility of mind, and with many tears, and temptations"* (v. 19).

# GLEANINGS FROM THE BOOK OF RUTH

**Tears of affection:** But Paul went on to identify with tears of affection, saying, *"I ceased not to warn every one night and day with tears"* (v. 31).

**Tears of affection:** As Paul left the Ephesian elders it is said that, *"they all wept sore, and fell on Paul's neck, and kissed him, Sorrowing most of all...that they should see his face no more"* (vv. 37-38).

## The Thought of Cleaving

Cleaving is an important aspect displayed in Ruth chapter 1. In fact, there is a pattern when all four chapters are considered together.

In chapter 1 **Ruth is cleaving**. Orpah leaves to go back to Moab, but Ruth cleaves to her mother-in-law.

In chapter 2 **Ruth is continuing**. When she is gleaning in the field, the servants point out to Boaz that Ruth has continued from morning until then, save for a short rest in the house.

In chapter 3 **Ruth is cleansing**. She washes and anoints herself and puts on the appropriate raiment.

In chapter 4 **Ruth gets compensation**. Ruth moves in a path that is contrary to nature, and is rewarded—she is compensated for it.

In chapter 1 Ruth's cleaving is tested in a threefold way;

There is **the pull for home**. *"Go, return each to her mother's house: the Lord deal kindly with you, as ye have dealt with the dead, and with me"* (v. 8).

There are **the perplexities of life**. *"Turn again, my daughters, go your way; for I am too old to have an husband. If I should say, I have hope, if I should have an husband also to night, and should also bear sons; Would ye tarry for them till they were grown? would you stay for them from having husbands? Nay, my daughters"* (vv. 12-13).

## Ruth Cleaving to Naomi

There is **the pattern of others**. *"Behold, thy sister in law is gone back unto her people, and unto her gods: return thou after thy sister in law"* (v. 15).

## The Thought of Receiving

When Naomi (and Ruth) return, the whole city is moved. The women say, *"Is this Naomi?"* (v. 19). Is this the woman who left us ten years ago? It is love that welcomes, and it is love that receives.

If it was a famine that took them away, it is the thought of bread that brings them back. That is what brought the prodigal son back from the far country. The prodigal said to himself, *"How many hired servants of my father's have bread enough and to spare, and I perish with hunger!"* (Luke 15:17). In like manner, Naomi responds to the news that the Lord had given his people bread in her own homeland.

The book of Jeremiah highlights the relationship between backsliding and recovery. Backsliding is getting away from God, and Jeremiah mentions it nine times (it appears three times in the book of Hosea), and it can be summarized in three steps:

> The **cause of backsliding**. *"My people have committed two evils; they have forsaken me the fountain of living water, and hewed them out cisterns, broken cisterns, that can hold no water"* (Jer. 2:13).
>
> The **cost of backsliding**. The lion slays, the wolf spoils and the leopard slaughters (Jer. 5:6).
>
> The **cure for backsliding**. *"Return, ye backsliding children, and I will heal your backslidings"* (Jer. 3:22).

Failure with God is never final, as David knew when he said, *"Let us fall now into the hand of the Lord; for his mercies are great: and let me not fall into the hand of man"* (2 Sam. 24:14). David knew he would receive more mercy from God than from man.

That backsliding can lead to recovery is illustrated in many places.

**The recovery of a brother.** Abraham brought back all the goods and *"brought again his brother Lot"* (Gen. 14:16).

**The recovery of a nazarite.** Samson's hair, that was shaven, began to grow again (Judg. 16:22).

**The recovery of a king.** After a rebuke, Jehoshaphat went out again among the people and *"brought them back unto the Lord God of their fathers"* (2 Chron. 19:4).

**The recovery of a sister.** Naomi says that she went out full but the Lord has brought her *"home again empty"* (Ruth 1:21).

This is all illustrated in Ruth chapter one, where there is **returning,** on the part of Naomi, and **receiving,** on the part of those in Bethlehem-Judah. I like that little word, *"again"* — it brings in the thought of recovery, as in all the examples given above.

# Chapter Two

# RUTH GLEANING IN THE FIELD

This chapter is dominated by lessons relating to the "field of Boaz". Since this is a type of the place belonging to Christ there is much to be learned from the illustration. Beginning with general gleanings from chapter two, we go on to a specific highlight on the field of Boaz and conclude with four practical lessons suggested from the application. This forms the outline of this section.

Gleanings from Ruth chapter two

Highlight: "The Field Belonging to Boaz"

Four Practical Teachings about "The Field"

## Gleanings from Ruth Chapter Two

A consideration of significant contrasts of chapter 2 with the previous chapter reveals some important lessons. Likewise, there being a number of important verbal interchanges in this chapter, a study of those who speak and what they say, can be very profitable, so we will view **"contrasts"** and significant **"speakings"**.

### Contrasts between Chapters One and Two

There is a vast contrast between Ruth chapter 1 and Ruth chapter 2.

In chapter 1 there are **two famines.** There is a famine in Bethlehem-Judah and there is a famine in Moab, and the famine of Moab far exceeds the famine of Judah. Naomi

49

admits such when she says she went out full but the Lord has brought her home again empty.

In chapter 2 there is **no thought of a famine**, for it is barley harvest and wheat harvest.

In chapter 1 there is a **dissatisfied woman**—as seen in Naomi, who says she went out full but came back empty.

In chapter 2 there is a **satisfied woman**, who ate and was sufficed.

In chapter 1 there are individuals who are **doing that which is right in their own eyes**. Elimelech, who leaves Bethlehem-Judah for Moab, Mahlon who marries Ruth, Chilion who marries Orpah, and Orpah who goes back to her country, her people and her gods.

In chapter 2 there are individuals **doing that which is right in the eyes of the Lord**.

In chapter 1 is the **government of God**. Naomi admits that the Almighty had dealt very bitterly with her.

In chapter 2 is the **grace of God**. *"Why have I found grace in thine eyes?"* (v. 10).

## "Speaking"

How forceful are right words. *"A word fitly spoken is like apples of gold in pictures of silver"* (Prov. 25:11). With so many illustrations, this is a "chapter of speaking".

> **Naomi speaks to Ruth** about Boaz. (Although we are not told this in so many words, it is a fairly safe assumption that, in a small village, Ruth would learn this from Naomi.) He is described as a mighty man of wealth, a man of valour who is outstanding in his character, and of great influence. He is a worthy man and a well to do man.
>
> **Ruth speaks to Naomi.** She mentions going to anyone's field, a landowner in whose sight she may find grace (v. 2).
>
> **Naomi speaks to Ruth.** *"Go, my daughter"* (v. 2).

# Ruth Gleaning in the Field

**Boaz speaks to the reapers.** *"The Lord be with you"* (v. 4).

**The reapers speak to Boaz.** *"The Lord bless thee"* (v. 4).

**Boaz speaks to the servant set over the reapers.** He asks who Ruth is. *"Whose damsel is this?"* (v. 5).

**The servant speaks to Boaz.** He tells Boaz who she is, where she is from, whom she came with and how long she had gleaned in the field (vv. 6-7).

**Boaz speaks to Ruth.** He gives her guidance for her feet, *"Go not to glean in another field"* (v. 8), gives her company (companions) to enjoy, *"Abide here fast by my maidens"* (v. 8) and gives her nourishment, provision and refreshment for her need (v. 9). Then he adds preservation.

**Boaz speaks to the young men.** He tells them to touch her not and rebuke her not (or reproach her not) (vv. 9, 15).

**Ruth speaks to Boaz.** *"Why have I found grace in thine eyes?"* (v. 10).

**Boaz speaks to Ruth.** He talks about the work she has done, about the step of faith she has taken, how she has left her father and mother and the land of her nativity to come to a people she did not know before (v. 11).

**Ruth and Naomi speak** about Boaz. *"The man is near of kin unto us, one of our next kinsmen"* (v. 20).

## Highlight: The Field Belonging to Boaz

The fields in the book of Ruth, in this picture before us, are interesting. There are two fields, and Ruth is moving from one to another.

> The field in chapter 1: The country of Moab could be read as, **the field of Moab.** This field answers to the field of Matthew 13. Moab is the world (v. 38).
>
> The field in chapter 2: **The field belonging unto Boaz.** This field answers to the field of 1 Corinthians 3. *"Ye are God's husbandry"* (v. 9). Believers are seen as God's cultivated field.

# GLEANINGS FROM THE BOOK OF RUTH

When Ruth moves from the field of Moab to the field of Bethlehem-Judah, she is moving in a new sphere, where the field belonging to Boaz plays a large role, both physically and spiritually. There is much to be learned along the way. Starting with the properties of the **field** itself, we consider the **Lord** (or owner) of the field and the pictures of the **Godhead** seen there. There is practical help (**care**) to be had in the field too. Finally, we can learn by considering things that are **not found** in the field.

## "The" Field

Notice what the field is to Ruth. There is everything that Ruth needs in the field belonging to Boaz.

> **The field is a place of counsel.** Ruth is told what to do, and she is told what not to do. *"Go not to glean in another field ..... Let thine eyes be on the field that they do reap, and go thou after them"* (vv. 8-9). She is told where to go, and she is told where not to go. *"Neither go from hence, but abide here fast by my maidens"* (v. 8).
>
> **The field is a place of comfort.** There is comfort for Ruth in the field belonging to Boaz. *"Thou hast comforted me, and for that thou hast spoken friendly unto thine handmaid, though I be not like unto one of thine handmaidens"* (v. 13).
>
> **The field is a place of compensation.** Ruth is compensated in the field. *"The Lord recompense thy work, and a full reward be given thee of the Lord the God of Israel, under whose wings thou art come to trust"* (v. 12).
>
> **The field is a place of companions.** It is in the field she finds her companions. *"Abide here fast by my maidens"* (v. 8). *"Go out with his maidens, that they meet thee not in any other field"* (v. 22).
>
> **The field is a place of care.** It is evident that the servant set over the reapers cares for her, for he knows every thing about her. Likewise, it is evident that Boaz cares about her. (This thought is further developed below, under "Care in the Field").

# Ruth Gleaning in the Field

## The Lord of the Field

The Lord of the field in Bethlehem-Judah is Boaz. He is lord and master of the field. As lord he will have no rivals, and as master he must be obeyed. In the book of Ruth, the privileged person is Ruth and the prominent person is Naomi, but the preeminent person is Boaz. He is a picture, a type of Christ, in that in all things he must have the pre-eminence.

Boaz says to the reapers, *"The Lord be with you"* (v. 4). He wishes the Lord to be with them in **guidance**, in **preservation**, in **strength** and in **provision**. In return the reapers say to Boaz, *"The Lord bless thee"* (v. 4). They wish for him the **enrichment of the Lord**, that the Lord would give him a **good harvest**.

It says about Ruth that, *"her hap was to light on a part of the field belonging unto Boaz"* (v. 3). "It happened" is the thought, but I don't think this was by chance or by accident. Overall, God is in control, and He ordered it so that Ruth arrives at the field of Boaz. The Lord rewards this woman for what she did - she finds protection in the Lord Jehovah. In the same way that the reapers speak about blessing Boaz, Naomi speaks about the Lord blessing him. *"Blessed be he of the Lord"* (v. 20).

**Lordship** is an important principle. Four people in the New Testament speak about the Lord Jesus being their Lord.

Notice **who** they are:

> **Elisabeth:** *"That the mother of my Lord should come to me"* (Luke 1:43).
>
> **Mary:** *"They have taken away my Lord* (out of the tomb), *and I know not where they have laid him"* (John 20:13).
>
> **Thomas:** *"My Lord and my God"* (John 20:28).
>
> **Paul:** *"Yea doubtless, and I count all things but loss for the excellency of the knowledge of Christ Jesus my Lord: for whom I have suffered the loss of all things"* (Phil. 3:8).

Notice **where** they are:

> **Elisabeth** is in her home.
>
> **Mary** is standing by the tomb.

**Thomas** is in the upper room and **Paul** is in prison. Notice **what** marks them:

**Elisabeth** is filled with the Spirit.
**Mary** is filled with sorrow.
**Thomas** is filled with doubt.
**Paul** is filled with joy and rejoicing.

Proving to us it is not what we have to live **on** that brings joy and contentment, but what we have to live **for**. Paul could say, *"For to me to live is Christ, and to die is gain"* (Phil. 1:21). In other words, to die is just more of Christ. The Lord Himself said, *"If I then, your Lord and Master, have washed your feet; ye also ought to wash one another's feet"* (John 13:14).

> I am the Lord's! yet teach me all it meaneth,
> All it involves of love and loyalty,
> Of holy service, full and glad surrender,
> And unreserved obedience unto Thee.

## Pictures of the Godhead in the "Field"

In Ruth chapter 2 we can see the Godhead—the Father, the Son and the Holy Spirit—linked with the field; a picture of the Godhead linked with the church.

**God** is mentioned in the chapter time and again.

**A picture of Christ is seen in Boaz.** A mighty man of wealth and a mighty man of valour, Boaz is the kinsman redeemer. His name means, "In Him is Strength", and he is a man of outstanding character. He is the lord and master of the field. This takes our minds to John 13, where the Lord says, *"Ye call me Master and Lord: and ye say well; for so I am. If I then, your Lord and Master, have washed your feet; ye also ought to wash one another's feet"* (John 13:13-14).

We should never forget who Christ is—He is Lord and Saviour. We have to grow in grace and in the knowledge of our Lord and Saviour Jesus Christ, for He is Lord and Christ.

## Ruth Gleaning in the Field

God has made this same Jesus who was crucified both Lord and Christ. He is Lord and Master. Thomas' words, *"my Lord and my God,"* are telling.

> As Lord and **Saviour** we appreciate Him.
> As Lord and **Christ** we exalt Him.
> As Lord and **Master** we obey Him.
> As Lord and **God** we worship Him.

**The Holy Spirit is seen in the servant set over the reapers.** The Servant knows all about Ruth.

> The Servant knows who she is.
> The Servant knows where she has come from.
> The Servant knows whom she came back with.
> The Servant knows the petition she asked.
> The Servant knows how long she was in the field.

### Care in the Field

The field is the place of shelter—the opposite of abandonment. Those in God's field care for one another, just as the servant over the reapers, and Boaz himself, watches out for Ruth when she is in the field. You no doubt have heard the expression, "Who cares?" as if no one cares. The Lord cares, but often we are like the disciples, who said to the Lord Jesus, *"Carest thou not that we perish?"* (Mark 4:38). And we are like Martha, who said to the Lord Jesus, *"Dost thou not care?"* (Luke 10:40).

> **God cares.** He says to cast *"all your care upon him; for he careth for you"* (1 Pet. 5:7). We are told what to do and we are told what not to do. It is God's will that I should cast my care on Him each day, but He also asks me not to cast my confidence away. *"Cast not away therefore your confidence, which hath great recompense of reward"* (Heb. 10:35). But oh how foolishly I act when, taken unawares, I cast away my confidence and I carry all my cares. Christ Jesus cares. There is a shepherd living

there, the firstborn from the dead, who tends with sweet unwearied care the flock for which he bled.

**The Holy Spirit cares.** *"He shall give you another Comforter, that he may abide with you for ever"* (John 14:16).

**The godly elder cares.** *"If a man know not how to rule his own house, how shall he take care of the church of God?"* (1 Tim. 3:5). And remember, we have to have the same care one for another.

## What is Not Found in the Field

It is important to notice what is not found in the field, and to learn from what is missing. In the field of Boaz there is no strife and no evil speaking.

### *There is No Strife in the Field of Boaz*

At the assembly at Corinth there was envy, strife and division. Similarly, there was biting and the devouring one of another at Galatia. There is nothing like that in the field belonging to Boaz. Envy and strife produce contention and every evil work. Proverbs speaks of the kind of people that sow, stir and kindle strife. These are the froward man, the angry man, the proud man and the talebearer – the ones that sow strife.

### *Have You Ever Noticed Where Strife is Found in the Bible?*

**Among the Herdsmen:** There was strife between the herdsmen of Abraham and Lot (Gen. 13:7).

**Among the City Dwellers:** David saw strife and violence in the city (Ps. 55:9).

**Among the Disciples:** There was strife among the disciples as to who would be the greatest (Luke 22:24).

**Among the Assembly:** There was envy, strife and division in the assembly at Corinth (1 Cor. 3:3). Paul said, *"Let nothing be done through strife and vainglory"* (Phil. 2:3). Strife is putting a brother down, while vain glory is raising oneself up.

# Ruth Gleaning in the Field

*There is No Evil Speaking in the Field of Boaz*

The Psalmist stressed the dangers of evil among God's people. *"Depart from evil, and do good; seek peace, and pursue it"* (Ps. 34:14).

**We can be evil in our thoughts:** *"Every imagination of the thoughts of his heart was only evil continually"* (Gen. 6:5).

**We can be evil in our hearts:** *"Take heed .... lest there be in any of you an evil heart of unbelief, in departing from the living God"* (Heb. 3:12).

**We can be evil in our words:** Speak not evil. *"Let no corrupt communication proceed out of your mouth, but that which is good to the use of edifying, that it may minister grace unto the hearers"* (Eph. 4:29). The world hated the Lord because He testified its deeds were evil.

**We can be evil in our company:** *"Be not deceived: evil communications* (or "companionship") *corrupt good manners"* (1 Cor. 15:33).

For evil behaviour, the Lord smote three people with leprosy; Gehazi, Uzziah and Miriam. Gehazi the **servant**, Uzziah the **sovereign**, and Miriam the **sister**.

**He smote Gehazi because of lies.** Gehazi lied to Naaman, to Elisha, and to God. We should keep in mind that Gehazi the liar became Gehazi the leper.

**He smote Uzziah for moving out his sphere.** God has a path for each one of us to move in, a work for each one of us to do, and a place for each one of us to fill.

**He smote Miriam because of evil speaking.** James warns us, *"Speak not evil one of another, brethren"* (Jas. 4:11) and the example of Anna is set before us, she who spake of Him to all (Luke 2:38).

Lying is particularly hateful to God. Among the six things (yea, seven) listed in Proverbs 6 that God hates, and that are an abomination to him, are a **lying tongue** and a **false witness that utters lies.** Those are included in the seven things that are hateful to God, hurtful to man and harmful to self. What was the sin of the old prophet in 1 Kings 13? He lied. And what was the sin of Ananias and Sapphira? They lied, and not to men, but to God (Acts 5).

## Four Practical Teachings about "The Field"

There are practical lessons to be learned from the characteristics of the field of Boaz. Lessons that apply to the assembly and that affect our daily walk with the Lord.

> The field is **a place of separation.**
> The field is **a place of activity.**
> The field is **a place of unity.**
> The field is **a place of purity.**

### A Place of Separation

**Boaz says to Ruth**, *"Go not to glean in another field"* (Ruth 2:8). He knows there are other fields apart from his. Since Boaz is a type of Christ, the fields other than his own would be the world.

> Are we cruising with this world?
> Are we courting this world?
> Are we conquering this world?
> Are we floating with this world?
> Are we flirting with this world?
> Are we fighting this world?
> Are we conformed to this world, or are we transformed?
> Are we going against the tide, or are we floating with the tide?

**The Call of the Lord is**, *"Come out from among them, and be ye separate"* (2 Cor. 6:17). We should be different; where God puts a difference we should keep that difference. The Lord put a difference between the Egyptians and Israel, between the innocent and the guilty, and between the precious and the vile.

## Ruth Gleaning in the Field

Notice three ways mentioned in the book of First Thessalonians that we should be different from this world:

**Let us not sleep:** We should not be as others, but should watch and be sober. Sleep, which is carnal indifference to spiritual things, should not mark us as the people of God (1 Thess. 5:6).

**Let us not sorrow:** We are not as others which have no hope (1 Thess. 4:13). The sorrow that marks the world should not mark us as the people of God.

**Let us not sin:** The sin that marks this world should not mark us as God's people. *"Not in the lust of concupiscence, even as the Gentiles which know not God"* (1 Thess. 4:5).

**The principle of separation** is illustrated in the story of the ten virgins. They were **different at the beginning,** for five were wise and five were foolish. They were **different at the end,** for the five wise went into the marriage and the door was shut, while the five foolish were left outside when the bridegroom came. But the tragedy was that there was **no difference in between!** They all slumbered and slept.

We have to be **righteous** in a scene of lawlessness.

We have to **shine** as lights in a scene of darkness.

We have to be **blameless** and **harmless** in the midst of a crooked and perverse generation.

In separation we can be as clear as ice - but we can also be as cold as ice.

There is a separation **from** and there is a separation **to**. Israel was to be separated **from** the world. God said, *"I am the Lord your God, which have separated you from other people"* (Lev. 20:24). The believer today is to be separated **to** God. *"Let us go forth therefore unto him without the camp, bearing his reproach"* (Heb. 13:13). We have no abiding city down here, but we seek one to come.

The tragedy of the day is that the church is so worldly and the world is so churchy that it is difficult to know the difference! There is no trouble with a ship in the water; the trouble begins when the water comes into the ship. Likewise, there is no trouble with the church in the world, but the trouble comes when the world comes into the church.

We were taught as young Christians to be separated from this world in every shape and form.

> We are to be separate from **Egypt**: with its treasure and pleasure.
>
> We are to be separate from **Sodom:** with its vice.
>
> We are to be separate from **Babylon:** with its music.
>
> We are to be separate from **Moab:** with its pride.

## A Place of Activity

There is activity in the field. They are not all doing the same thing, but they are all doing something. Notice that each one is doing their part:

> **Boaz, the lord and master of the field:** He is the one who gives commands and orders.
>
> **The servant set over the reapers:** He has a watchful eye.
>
> **The reapers and the gleaners**. The reapers in the harvest are those who cut down, while the gleaners are those who pick up. Both are needed.

This is in line with the assembly responsibilities mentioned in 1 Corinthians 12, in which are highlighted three things:

> **God does not intend one man to do everything.** The body is not one member, but many. God hates the system of clerisy. God hates a one man band.
>
> **God does not intend every man to do the same thing.** Are all apostles? No. Are all prophets? No. Are all teachers? No.
>
> **God DOES intend every man to do something.** *"For to one is given by the Spirit the word of wisdom; to another the word of knowledge"* (1 Cor. 12:8).

## Ruth Gleaning in the Field

Some may have a nobler task than you, but you have your own work to do, and no one in all God's universe can do it as well as you. We can shun our responsibility, but we cannot shun the consequences of shunning our responsibility. The assembly could be a happier, healthier, holier place if each one would shoulder their responsibility. Is your place a large place?—tend it with care, for God put you there. Is your place a small place? —guard it with care, for God put you there. The most humble sister, in the most obscure position, is as precious and pleasing to the heart of God as the most gifted, godly brother.

There are three things we have to do continually. We have to:

**Continually seek God:** We have to seek the Lord, seek His strength, and seek His face continually.

**Continually sacrifice (or praise) to God:** We have to offer the sacrifice of praise and do it continually.

**Continually serve God:** It was to Daniel, *"Thy God whom thou servest continually"* (Dan. 6:16). We have to serve God with joy, with gladness, with sincerity, with truth, with reverence and with godly fear.

A model assembly is where everyone participates, none monopolize, and where everybody is somebody. Every one of us has a path to move in, a work to do and a place to fill.

**We have a path to move in.** Happy if it could be said of us, as it was said of Abraham's servant, *"I being in the way, the Lord led me"* (Gen. 24:27).

**We have a work to do.** Happy if it could be said of us, as was said of Nehemiah, *"I am doing a great work, so I cannot come down"* (Neh. 6:3). Or, as was said of Mary, *"She hath wrought a good work on me...She hath done what she could"* (Mark 14:6, 8).

**We have a place to fill.** Happy if it could be said of us, as it was said of David, *"David's place was empty"* (1 Sam. 20:25).

# GLEANINGS FROM THE BOOK OF RUTH

A Place of Unity

The field belonging to Boaz is a place of unity. It's nice to notice the harmony that exists in that field.

> **Boaz** says to the reapers, *"The Lord be with you"* (v. 4). The Lord be with you, guiding you, strengthening you, protecting you, providing for you.
>
> **The reapers** say to Boaz, *"The Lord bless thee"* (v. 4). The Lord bless you, enrich you, and give you a good harvest.
>
> **The young men** minister refreshment. Ruth is told, *"When thou art athirst…drink of that* (water) *which the young men have drawn"* (v. 9).

In the history of God's earthly people, Israel, time and again the nation is presented as being one man. This shows the oneness, the unity and the harmony marking them.

> **God's people are as one man in purpose.** They are seen, from Dan to Beersheba, *"knit together as one man"* (Judg. 20:11) illustrating the bond, the oneness and the unity that marked them.
>
> **God's people are as one man in worship.** We see them as one man building the altar sacrificing to God in Ezra chapter 3, verse 1.
>
> **God's people are as one man in ministry.** They gather as one man and it is as one man in ministry in Nehemiah chapter 8, verse 1.
>
> **God's people are as one man in the gospel** in the New Testament. We see the truth of the preaching of the gospel as one man. *"Stand fast in one spirit, with one mind striving together for the faith of the gospel"* (Phil. 1:27).

The thought of unity characterises the field of Boaz. The Psalmist could say, *"Behold, how good and how pleasant it is for brethren to dwell together in unity"* (Ps. 133:1). Unity is sweet, unity is strength, unity is salvation. We are never told to make unity - we are told to keep it. *"Endeavouring to keep the unity of the Spirit in the* (uniting) *bond of peace."* (Eph. 4:3).

## Ruth Gleaning in the Field

It is good and pleasant for brethren to dwell together in unity.

**Pleasant to God** - He planned it.

**Pleasant to Christ** - He died for it.

**Pleasant to the Spirit** - He makes it.

**Pleasant to angels** - They behold it.

**Pleasant to the world** - They admire it.

**Pleasant to the saints** - They enjoy it.

In the Scriptures we see that which is **good and acceptable** (or pleasing), that which is **good and profitable**, and that which is **good and pleasant**.

### A Place of Purity

God is not looking for people who are clever - God is looking for people who are clean. Those that bore the vessels of the Lord had to be clean. The field of Boaz is characterised by purity of action, as typified by the three things that Boaz says to the young men about their relation towards Ruth.

**Touch her not** (v. 9).

**Reproach her not** (v. 15).

**Rebuke her not** (v. 16).

Purity is associated with washing. This is very significant among God's earthly people, Israel, and, by application, to believers today. (This thought is more fully developed in section E: Ruth chapter 3, under "The Importance of Cleansing").

**Washing comes before worshipping:** Before you get the thought of worshipping you get the thought of washing. In Genesis 35, Jacob goes to Bethel to worship, and he said to his household and them that were with him, *"Put away the strange gods that are among you, and be clean, and change your garments"* (Gen. 35:2).

Before you worship God there are three things you must do. There must be **reality** (put away the strange gods) and there must be **purity** (be clean) and there must be **freshness** (change your garments before worship).

**Washing comes before work:** And before you get the thought of the warfare of the work in the book of Numbers, you get the thought of washing. *"Cleanse them ...let them wash their clothes, and so make themselves clean"* (Num. 8:7).

**Washing comes before witnessing:** In the gospel of John you have washing before witnessing in the church age. Washing (John 13:5) comes before witness (John 15:27).

**Washing comes before communion:** Ruth washes herself before communion. Before Ruth spends a night at the feet of Boaz she washes herself and anoints herself and puts her raiment upon her (Ruth 3:3).

Chapter Three

# RUTH LYING AT THE FEET

This chapter begins with the thought of rest and it closes with the thought of rest—a rest for Ruth and a rest for Boaz. While it is important that we labour in the field, it is likewise also important that we lie at His feet, and that is brought out in this chapter. The key setting of the passage is the threshing floor of Boaz. By way of comparison, the key settings in the four chapters of the book of Ruth are:

**A famine** in chapter 1: The famine in Moab.

**A field** in chapter 2: The field belonging unto Boaz.

**A floor** (a threshing floor) in chapter 3: The threshing floor of Boaz.

**A family** in chapter 4: The setting up of the family of Boaz and Ruth.

This outline is very straightforward and is based, as before, on gleanings and practical teachings:

Gleanings from Ruth chapter 3

Four Practical Truths about the believer's life

## Gleanings from Ruth Chapter Three

There are lessons to be learned from the story of chapter 3. Here we follow the narrative as it tells of important **characteristics** which mark Ruth, lessons to be learned from the godly man, Boaz, doing his own **winnowing,** the significance of **fellowship with Boaz** and the promise of **rest** to come.

# GLEANINGS FROM THE BOOK OF RUTH

## Characteristic Marks of Ruth

Testimony to Ruth's holy character is made in chapter 3, but it is good to review what marks this woman in previous parts of the book.

> **She has a stedfast mind.** *"When she saw that she was stedfastly minded to go with her, then she left speaking unto her"* (Ruth 1:18).
>
> **She has a tender spirit.** She lifts up her voice and she weeps in Ruth 1, verse 9.
>
> **She has a kind heart.** *"The Lord deal kindly with you, as ye have dealt with the dead, and with me"* (Ruth 1:8).
>
> **She has a subjective will.** She goes where she is sent and she does as she is commanded, like her Lord who said, *"Not my will, but thine, be done"* (Luke 22:42).
>
> **She has willing and working hands.** She gleans, beats out what she has gleaned, takes it up and gives to another.
>
> In that she is a picture of one who gleans in the Word of God. She **gleans** (which is like reading*)*, **beats out** that which she has gleaned (this is like meditating), she **takes it up** (she applies it to herself), and then **gives it forth** (she shares with others). Henry Pickering was once asked, "What is the best use of the Bible?" He said, "Read it through, note it down, pray it in, live it out and pass it on." This is the thought behind Ruth's gleaning.
>
> **She has a holy character.** *"All the city of my people doth know that thou art a virtuous woman"* (Ruth 3:11).

Her name means **beauty** or **satisfied.** There is a beauty that will go with you as far as the grave but no further, but there is a beauty that is moral, spiritual and eternal. That is the beauty that marks Ruth.

## Winnowing

Winnowing is the work of separating the wheat from the chaff. It is not the same thing as threshing, which is the process

## Ruth Lying at the Feet

of loosening the grain from the ear and the straw. Threshing is a work that needs to be done by force, and oxen or threshing machines are used. Winnowing means "to clean", that chaff and dust are taken away, and has a spiritual application. I am thinking of its importance regarding our thought life in that sense, whether they be heavenly thoughts (sober thoughts, right thoughts) or evil thoughts (the work of Satan).

> The Lord wants to **keep the wheat and get rid of the chaff**. God does not want the chaff; that He reserves for the unquenchable fire (Matt. 3:12).
>
> Satan wants to **get rid of the wheat and keep the chaff**. Since he knows he cannot destroy us, he wants to sift us to **disgrace** us, to **depress** us, and to **defeat** us (Luke 22:31).

It is better to be winnowed by Christ than to be sifted by Satan.

### Fellowship with Boaz

The scene having been set in the first two chapters, the third chapter focuses on fellowship with Boaz. Ruth spends a night at his feet. Before that, however, she had to prepare herself to meet Boaz and to be acceptable to him.

> **Ruth's protection is God** in chapter 2. *"Under whose wings thou art come to trust"* (v. 12).
>
> **Ruth's protection is Boaz** in chapter 3. *"Spread therefore thy skirt over thine handmaid"* (v. 9). The only safeguard against backsliding is communion with Christ. *"Abide thou with me, fear not: for he that seeketh my life seeketh thy life: but with me thou shalt be in safeguard"* (1 Sam. 22:23).
>
> **Boaz counsels Ruth** in chapter 2. He tells her where to go and he tells her where not to go. Remember that in the multitude of counsellors there is safety (Prov. 11:14).
>
> **Boaz comforts Ruth** in chapter 2. *"Thou hast comforted me, and for that thou hast spoken friendly unto thine handmaid"* (v. 13). The thought is, "to the heart of thy handmaid".
>
> **Boaz commends Ruth** in chapter 3. *"Blessed be thou of the Lord, my daughter...For all the city of my people doth know that thou art a virtuous woman"* (vv. 10-11).

**Boaz compensates Ruth** in chapter 3. He measures six measures of barley (v. 15).

**Boaz completes Ruth** in chapter 4. She finds her completeness in Boaz, a picture of the believer in Christ. *"For in him* (Christ) *dwelleth all the fullness of the Godhead bodily...And ye are complete in him"* (Col. 2:9-10).

All this is what Ruth has been brought into:

In chapter 1 **Ruth is returning and resolving.**

In chapter 2 **Ruth is serving and reaping.**

In chapter 3 **Ruth is resting and receiving.**

In chapter 4 **Ruth is being related through redemption.**

## Rest

Rest is like any other word we read about in the Bible—it must be taken in the context in which it is found.

**There is a rest of conscience.** This is when we rest where God rests in the finished work of Christ. We have responded to the teaching of Matthew 11:28, *"Come unto me, all ye that labour and are heavy laden, and I will give you rest."*

**There is a future rest.** *"There remaineth therefore a rest to the people of God"* (Heb. 4:9). *"In my Father's house are many mansions* (or resting places): *if it were not so, I would have told you. I go to prepare a place for you"* (John 14:2). Like Israel of old, we have a rest in view, secure from adverse power. Like them we pass through a desert—for Israel's God is our God.

**There is a present rest.** *"Come ye yourselves apart into a desert place, and rest a while"* (Mark 6:31).

In Ruth chapter 3 it is **matrimonial rest**. It has been well said it takes money to build a house, but it takes love to build the home. Where love is shown and subjection is shown, rest will be enjoyed.

## Ruth Lying at the Feet

# Four Practical Truths about the Believer's Life

In chapter 3 of the book of Ruth we can notice four important truths that have very practical applications.

> **The truth of being clean (cleansing).** Ruth is told to wash herself before going to see Boaz.
>
> **The truth of communion.** Ruth spends one night at the feet of Boaz.
>
> **The truth of consecration.** Ruth says to Boaz, *"I am Ruth thy handmaid"* (v. 9). In the sense of the Redeemer, she is saying, "Thou canst have all thou wilt of me."
>
> **The truth of commendation.** *"For all the city of my people doth know that thou art a virtuous woman"* (v. 11).

## The Importance of Cleansing

Ruth's preparation for the meeting with Boaz is the subject of verses 1 to 7. *"Wash thyself therefore, and anoint thee, and put thy raiment upon thee"* (v. 3).

Paul, after he saw sinners saved and an assembly planted, was interested in the salvation, the safety and the state of the people of God, which would include cleansing. This is seen in Paul's letter to the Philippians.

> **Salvation.** In chapter 2 of the Philippian epistle, Paul told them to work out their own salvation with fear and trembling (v. 12). This is the salvation of the assembly from strife, envy and division.
>
> **Safety.** In the third chapter Paul said, *"To write the same things to you, to me indeed is not grievous, but for you it is safe"* (Phil. 3:1).
>
> **State.** Paul sent Timothy to Philippi that he might be of good comfort when he knew their state—the thought expressed in the Proverbs. *"Be thou diligent to know the state of thy flocks, and look well to thy herds"* (Prov. 27:23).

# GLEANINGS FROM THE BOOK OF RUTH

## The Importance of Washing

The thought of washing is a very important truth in the Scriptures, because it comes before communion. We are living in a cold, callus, crooked, corrupt world. There may be a young Christian and you are asking yourself the question, "How can I be clean in such an unclean world?" The old sister was right when she said, "This book will keep you from sin and sin will keep you from this book." The Psalmist said the same thing. *"Wherewithal shall a young man cleanse his way? by taking heed thereto according to thy word"* (Ps. 119:9).

The believer keeps in mind that within the believer's body is the Holy Spirit, who can be grieved and quenched, and keeps in mind that any moment the Lord could come. *"Every man that hath this hope in him purifieth himself, even as he is pure"* (1 John 3:3). Our minds should be on right things—heavenly things—and our minds set on things above, where Christ is seated at the right hand of God.

Holy men and holy women have to handle holy things, and holy men of God speak as they are moved by the Holy Spirit.

**Holy men** pray, lifting up holy hands, without wrath or doubting.

**A holy priesthood** offers up spiritual sacrifice.

**A holy nation** shows forth the excellences of Him that called us out of darkness into His marvellous light.

**Washing,** symbolic in God's Word of personal cleansing, appears in a distinct priority in Scriptures. **Washing** comes before **worship,** before **witnessing,** before **warfare** and before **waiting.** (This is a development of the practical thoughts already presented in our discussion of Ruth chapter 2, under "A Place of Purity" in Section D).

*Washing Comes before Worship.*

Consider the examples of Jacob and David before they went to worship.

**Jacob.** Before he went up to El-Bethel to worship, Jacob told his household there had to be a covering up and a cleaning up. *"Put away the strange gods that are among you, and be clean, and change your garments"* (Gen. 35:2). God is looking for reality, and he is looking for purity and freshness.

**David.** Likewise, David showed the same care. *"David arose from the earth, and washed, and anointed himself, and changed his apparel, and came into the house of the Lord, and worshiped"* (2 Sam. 12:20).

*Washing Comes before Witnessing.*

This is especially shown in John's gospel. In John 13 there is the thought of washing. Notice this in three different ways.

**The washing of regeneration:** Washed all over.

**The washing of renewal (or reunion):** If I wash thee not.

**The washing of responsibility.** Wash one another's feet.

*Washing Comes before Warfare.*

Numbers 8 is about the Levites' preparation. They were to wash their clothes and cleanse themselves (v. 7). Then, we read, *"To wait upon the service of the tabernacle of the congregation"* (v. 24). In the RV this reads, *"to war the warfare in the work"*—so there is a link between washing and warfare.

The teaching of 1 Peter 2 is very important regarding cleansing, and the link between cleansing and warfare is made once again. *"Abstain from fleshly lusts, which war against the soul"* (1 Pet. 2:11). A valuable principle is illustrated by a sequence of truths that are revealed in order:

**The thought of growing up.** *"As newborn babes, desire the sincere milk of the word, that ye may grow thereby"* (1 Pet. 2:2).

**The thought of being built up.** *"Ye also, as lively stones, are built up a spiritual house"* (1 Pet. 2:5).

**The thought of offering up.** *"An holy priesthood, to offer* up spiritual sacrifices, acceptable to God by Jesus Christ" (1 Pet. 2:5).

**The thought of showing forth.** *"That ye should shew forth the praises of him who hath called you"* (1 Pet. 2:9).

But before you get all that truth there is **the thought of cleaning up.** *"Wherefore laying aside all malice, and all guile, and hypocrisies, and envies, and all evil speakings"* (1 Pet. 2:1).

*Washing Comes before Waiting.*

In the third chapter Ruth washes before waiting. Ruth is waiting, but before that she has to wash herself, anoint herself, and put her raiment upon her. It is the difference between our standing and our state.

> Our standing is what we are in Christ, our state is what we are in the Lord.
>
> In our standing we have been washed. In our state we have to be washed.
>
> *"And such were some of you: but ye are washed, but ye are sanctified, but ye are justified"* (1 Cor. 6:11).
>
> > **Washed** - made clean.
> >
> > **Sanctified** - made holy.
> >
> > **Justified** - made righteous.
>
> *"Not by works of righteousness which we have done, but according to his mercy he saved us, by the washing of regeneration, and renewing of the Holy Ghost"* (Titus 3:5).

The truth is that, whether it be Old Testament or New Testament, it is holy men and holy women that handle holy things. In the books of Samuel three types of men wear the linen ephod, which speaks of purity.

> **Samuel the prophet** is girded with a linen ephod.
>
> **David the king** is girded with a linen ephod.
>
> **The priests of the Lord** were girded with the linen ephod.

## Ruth Lying at the Feet

*What is the Lesson of Washing?*

**If I am going to speak for God** (as seen in the **prophet**) I must be pure, I must be clean, I must be holy.

**If I am going to rule for God** (as seen in the **king**) I must be pure, clean and holy.

**If I am going to worship God** (as seen in the **priest**) I must be pure, clean and holy.

It is men who lift up holy hands without wrath or doubting that pray. It is **holy men of God** who speak moved by the Holy Spirit (2 Pet. 1:21). *"Holiness becometh thine house, O Lord, forever"* (Ps. 93:5).

It is a **holy nation** that shows forth the excellency of *"him who hath called you out of darkness into his marvellous light"* (1 Pet. 2:9).

It's a **holy priesthood** that offers spiritual sacrifices (1 Pet. 2:5).

Three times you read about a godly man in the Psalms.

**The value of a godly man.** *"The Lord hath set apart him that is godly for himself"* (Ps. 4:3).

**The privilege of a godly man.** *"Every one that is godly (shall) pray unto thee in a time when thou mayest be found"* (Ps. 32:6).

**The scarceness of a godly man.** *"Help, Lord; for the godly man ceaseth; for the faithful fail from among the children of men"* (Ps. 12:1).

## The Importance of Communion

When we think of communion we think of sharing, fellowship, intimacy, oneness and togetherness. This is beautifully shown in the book of Ruth, beginning at the feet of Boaz. Notice the outcome of Ruth spending the night at the feet of Boaz.

The spot at the feet of Boaz was;

**A place of instruction.** *"He will tell thee what thou shalt do"* (v. 4).

**A place of rest.** *"Lie down until the morning. And she lay at his feet until the morning"* (vv. 13-14).

**A place of protection.** *"Spread therefore thy skirt over thine handmaid"* (v. 9).

**A place of promise.** *"I will do to thee all that thou requirest"* (v. 11).

**A place of provision.** Ruth receives far more at the feet of Boaz than she does in the field of Boaz. In the field she gathers handfuls - at his feet she is given lapfuls.

**A place of comfort.** Boaz says fear not (v. 11).

**A place of commendation.** *"Blessed be thou of the Lord, my daughter: for thou hast showed more kindness in the latter end than at the beginning"* (v. 10). *"For all the city of my people doth know that thou art a virtuous woman"* (v. 11).

**A place of compensation.** *"He measured six measures of barley, and laid it on her"* (v. 15).

Christianity is fellowship with God.

**Fellowship with the Father.** *"Truly our fellowship is with the Father, and with his Son Jesus Christ"* (1 John 1:3).

**Fellowship with the Son.** *"God is faithful, by whom ye were called unto the fellowship of his Son Jesus Christ our Lord"* (1 Cor. 1:9).

**Fellowship with the Holy Spirit.** There is fellowship (communion) with the Spirit, as seen in Philippians, *"If* (or since) *any fellowship of the Spirit"* (Phil. 2:1).

We live our lives the wrong way round. Whereas Christ lived with God and visited men, we live with men and visit God.

Think of the outcome of communion.

In the life of Moses it **made his face shine**. *"Moses wist* (knew) *not that the skin of his face shone while he talked with him"* (Ex. 34:29). Moses was not going about the camp saying, "Look, my face is shining." He knew not.

# Ruth Lying at the Feet

Oh for the shining of the face,
Oh for the ignorance of the shining.

In the life of Peter and John it **produced boldness.** *"When they saw the boldness of Peter and John, and perceived that they were unlearned and ignorant men...they took knowledge of them, that they had been with Jesus"* (Acts 4:13).

The woman who is most linked with the feet of Christ is Mary of Bethany.

**Mary at the feet of Christ in Luke 10.** She is there as a **learner**, she knows Christ as **prophet**.

**Mary at the feet of Christ in John 11.** She is there as a **mourner**, and knows Christ as **priest**.

**Mary at the feet of Christ in John 12.** She is there as a **worshipper**, and knows Christ as **King**.

It was while she was communing at the feet of Christ that Mary was criticized:

She is criticised by **Martha**. *"Bid her therefore that she help me"* (Luke 10:40).

She is criticised by **the disciples**. *"Why was this waste of the ointment made?"* (Mark 14:4).

She is criticised by **Judas**. *"Why was not this ointment sold for three hundred pence, and given to the poor?...Not that he cared for the poor"* (John 12:5-6).

The one who enjoyed **communion** and the one who was **criticized,** was the one who was **commended**. *"Mary hath chosen that good part, which shall not be taken away from her"* (Luke 10:42). *"Let her alone; why trouble ye her? She hath wrought a good work on me...She hath done what she could: she is come aforehand to anoint my body to the burying"* (Mark 14:6, 8).

**Order.** I would like you to notice an order of things in the Scriptures. In this case, the order is that communion comes before service.

# GLEANINGS FROM THE BOOK OF RUTH

In 1 Chronicles 4:23 the potters dwelt with the king for his work. They were having communion before his work-service. There is a time to be silent and a time to speak. Notice the order. There is a time to be silent, while God speaks to us, and then a time for us to speak for we speak for God.

> **Elijah.** God said to Elijah to go and hide himself - before he said to go and show himself.
>
> **The Disciples.** Christ chose 12 disciples that they might be with him—and then that He might send them forth to preach.
>
> **John the Baptist.** John was in the desert - until his showing to Israel.
>
> **The Lord.** The Lord Himself had a **private life with God,** a **public life for God,** and a **prayer life to God.**

Communion with God must always precede service for Him.

> **To walk with God no strength is lost:** walk on, walk on.
>
> **To walk with God no breath is lost:** talk on, talk on.
>
> **To wait on God no time is lost:** wait on, wait on.

Ruth's example is an illustration of communion.

Communion is associated with **fragrance, freshness and fruitfulness**, three things which marked Ruth and which ought to mark every Christian. These three things we see in Christ:

> **Christ is Fragrant.** *"All thy garments smell of myrrh, and aloes, and cassia"* (Ps. 45:8).

> Himself alone Thy heart could fill,
> Obedient ever to Thy will,
> And ever thy delight;
> No heart could know, no tongue express
> How fragrant in His preciousness,
> How pleasing in Thy sight.

> **Christ is always Fresh.** *"But I am like a green olive tree in the house of the God"* (Ps. 52:8).

# Ruth Lying at the Feet

**Christ is Fruitful.** *"Except a corn of wheat fall into the ground and die, it abideth alone: but if I die, it bringeth forth much fruit"* (John 12:24).

## The Importance of Consecration

Consecration carries with it the thought of **dedication**. It is the truth of Romans 12:1. *"That ye present your bodies a living sacrifice."*

In the privacy of the threshing floor, Ruth says to Boaz, *"I am Ruth thine handmaid"* (v. 9). In reply, Boaz says to Ruth, *"I will do to thee all that thou requirest"* (v. 11). This exchange could be read like this; "Thou could have all thou wilt of me." Ruth is saying, **I am Ruth thine handmaid, thou could have all thou wilt of me.**

We have to present our bodies a living sacrifice, holy, acceptable unto God, which is your reasonable service. God wants;

>Our **ears** to listen to Him.
>Our **hands** to work for Him.
>Our **heart** to love Him.
>Our **feet** to walk in His paths.

The story is told about an Indian woman that made her way to the Ganges River to offer a child to her god. She had a son that was strong and healthy and a son that was weak and sickly. And she takes the son that was strong and healthy and she offers him to her god. The next day she was met by a friend and asked why she presented the strong and healthy and not the weak and sickly. Her words were, **my god deserves the best.** Ye are bought with a price we are not our own. We have to glorify God in our body, and not become the bondservants of men.

### Consecration is for Today

Naomi's remark to Ruth (*"The man will not be in rest, until he have finished the thing this day"* — 3:18) draws our attention to the importance of the "todays of Scripture". There are a number of significant today's of Scripture, including the today of consecration;

**The today of salvation.** *"Today if ye will hear his voice, Harden not your heart"* (Ps. 95:7-8). *"This day is salvation come to this house"* (Luke 19:9).

So come to Christ; O, come today.

The Father, the Son and the Spirit say, come. And the bride repeats the call.

**The today of occupation.** *"Go work to day in my vineyard"* (Matt. 21:28).

**The today of meditation.** *"Where hast thou gleaned today? and where wroughtest thou?"* (Ruth 2:19).

**The today of consecration.** *"Who then is willing to consecrate his service this day unto the Lord?"* (1 Chron. 29:5) God does not want part of us - He wants all of us.

> Take my life, and let it be
> Consecrated, Lord to thee.

*Exhortation*

It is encouraging to think that you and I belong to the Lord.

**He is with us in temptation** - as with Joseph.

**He is with us in the trials of life** - as with Job.

**He is with us in the toils of life** - as with Jeremiah.

Not only is it encouraging but it is enriching. All things are yours, he tells us. *"Whether Paul, or Apollos, or Cephas, or the world, or life, or death, or things present, or things to come; all are yours; And ye are Christ's; and Christ is God's"* (1 Cor. 3:22 -23).

But it comes with a challenge.

> I am the Lord's! yet teach me all it meaneth,
> All it involves of love and loyalty,
> Of holy service, full and glad surrender,
> And unreserved obedience unto Thee.

# Ruth Lying at the Feet

## The Importance of Commendation

Commendation is important for it is an evaluation of a person's character. It is seen very much in the case of Ruth, who is very highly commended by all who know her. Boaz says of Ruth, *"All the city of my people doth know that thou art a virtuous woman"* (v. 11). In the place where we are known, in the home where we live, and in the assembly where we labour, it is important that we have a testimony.

Think of these examples of the important commendations that pertained to the Lord, to Samuel and to Samson.

> **The Lord:** The place where He was known was the place where He taught. *"And he came to Nazareth, where he had been brought up: and, as his custom was, he went into the synagogue on the sabbath day, and stood up for to read"* (Luke 4:16).
>
> He **opened** the book.
>
> He **read** the book.
>
> He **closed** the book.
>
> He **explained** the book. *"This day is this scripture fulfilled in your ears"* (Luke 4:21).
>
> **Samuel:** The place where he was known was the place where he judged, and where he built an altar. *"And his return was to Ramah; for there was his house; and there he judged Israel; and there he built an altar unto the Lord"* (1 Sam. 7:17). Samuel is linked with the city in the story of Saul and the lost asses, as being a man of God. *"There is in this city a man of God, and he is an honourable man; all that he saith cometh surely to pass"* (1 Sam. 9:6).
>
> **Samson: The place where he was known was the place where the Spirit of God moved him.** He was a Danite, and the Scriptures say about Samson that, *"The Spirit of the Lord began to move him at times in the camp of Dan"* (Judg. 13:25).

We are the only Bible the careless world will read.

We are the **sinner's gospel.**

We are the **scoffer's creed.**

We are **God's last message.**

Given in deed and in word. What if the print be crooked, and what if the type be blurred?

When we think of commendation we think of Christ.

**Heaven commended Christ.** *"Thou art my beloved Son, in whom I am well pleased"* (Mark 1:11).

**Earth commended Christ.** John the Baptist said of Him, My successor is my superior because He was my predecessor.

**Hell testified of Christ.** *"I know thee who thou art, the Holy one of God"* (Mark 1:24).

## Appeal

Timothy, whose name means "honouring God", knew about commendation. Does every Christian honour God? The answer is no. Every Christian should honour God but not everyone does.

**We either rob God, or we fear Him.** *"If then I be a father, where is mine honour? and if I be a master, where is my fear?"* (Mal. 1:6) and the thought of Malachi 1:14 is, if I be a great king where is my worship? *"I am a great King, saith the Lord of hosts"* (Mal. 1:14).

There were those in Malachi's day that robbed God, and there were those that feared him.

**We either seek God, or we forsake Him.** *"If thou seek him, he will be found of thee; but if thou forsake him, he will cast thee off for ever"* (1 Chron. 28:9).

**We either love God, or we hate Him.** *"No man can serve two masters: for either he will hate the one, and love the other; or else he will hold to the one, and despise the other. Ye cannot serve God and mammon"* (Matt. 6:24).

## Ruth Lying at the Feet

**We either glorify God or we grieve Him.** In Malachi we see God honoured and we see Him dishonoured. Those who robbed God - grieved Him; those who feared Him - glorified Him.

**We either honour God, or we despise Him.** *"Them that honour me I will honour, and they that despise me shall be lightly esteemed"* (1 Sam. 2:30).

# Chapter Four
# RUTH FRUITFUL IN MARRIAGE

As we consider the life of Ruth we can see it was not an easy road, but in chapter 4 there is a glorious ending to this beautiful book. This is a picture of the Christian for, likewise, we are not promised a smooth sailing. The Lord Jesus taught His own.

> *"If the world hate you, ye know that it hated me before it hated you"* (John 15:18).
>
> *"These things I have spoken unto you, that in me ye might have peace. In the world ye shall have tribulation"* (John 16:33).
>
> *"Yea, and all that will live godly in Christ Jesus shall suffer persecution"* (2 Tim. 3:12).

In the nearer kinsman Naomi and Ruth came up against refusal. While he was prepared to buy the land, the kinsman was not able to restore their inheritance. Boaz, on the other hand, was prepared to buy the field and purchase the pearl! The key persons in this chapter form the basis of this section, as outlined below:

Gleanings from Ruth chapter four

Four Practical Traits of Personalities in chapter four

## Gleanings from Ruth Chapter Four

By this time the scene is set, for changes have occurred, and there is much to delight. We highlight this by **contrasting** the start with the finish, by considering the **Lord's doings** in

# GLEANINGS FROM THE BOOK OF RUTH

the life of Ruth, Boaz and Naomi, and conclude with a focus on **serving**.

## Contrasts between Chapters One and Four

There is a vast contrast between Ruth chapter 1 and Ruth chapter 4. (This is complementary to the similar outline in *Gleanings from the Whole Book of Ruth* on page 13.)

> In chapter 1 we see **life taken.** The death of Elimelech, Mahlon and Chilion.
> In chapter 4 we see **life given.** The birth of Obed.

> In chapter 1 we see **marriages that are not of God.** The sons marry Moabites.
> In chapter 4 we see **a marriage that is of God.** Ruth marries Boaz.

> In chapter 1 we see **a backslider.** Elimelech leaves his inheritance.
> In chapter 4 we see **a brother.** Elimelech's name is restored among his brethren.

> In chapter 1 we see **a heart broken.** Naomi's.
> In chapter 4 we see **a heart delighted.** Naomi's.

> In chapter 1 we see **headship lost.** Seen in Elimelech.
> In chapter 4 we see **headship recovered.** Seen in Boaz.

> In chapter 1 we see **sonship lost.** Seen in Mahlon and Chilion.
> In chapter 4 we see **sonship recovered.** Seen in Obed.

> In chapter 1 we see **no king.**
> In chapter 4 we see **the best king.**

> In chapter 1 we see **a woman that was full and now is empty.** Naomi says she went out full but the Lord brought her home again empty.
>
>> She goes out knowing the grace of God, but comes back knowing the government of God.
>>
>> She goes out a wife, but comes back a widow.
>>
>> She goes out with two children, but comes back with no children.

## Ruth Fruitful in Marriage

> She goes out well known, but comes back unknown.

> In chapter 4 we see **a woman that was empty and now is full.** The women of the city say to Naomi, *"Thy daughter in law, which loveth thee, which is better to thee than seven sons, hath born him* (Obed)*"* (Ruth 4:15).

> In chapter 1 we see **perplexity.**
> In chapter 4 we see **peace.**

> In chapter 1 we see **barrenness.** Both Ruth and Orpah are barren.
> In chapter 4 we see **fruitfulness.** Verse 13 tells that Ruth bears a son, and the women, her neighbours, say, *"There is a son born to Naomi"* (v. 17).

When it is our way, it will land in **perplexity** and **barrenness.** When it is God's way it will end in **peace** and **fruitfulness.**

### The Lord's Doings

In the context of the marvellous way in which God has worked in the life of Ruth (and of Boaz and Naomi) we have before us the greatness of our God. *"Great is the Lord, and greatly to be praised; and his greatness is unsearchable"* (Ps. 145:3).

It is of vital importance that we see the Lord's doings in connection with Ruth in chapter 4.

> **Verse 11:** *"The Lord make the woman that is come into thine house like Rachel and like Leah."*
>
> **Verse 12:** *"Of the seed which the Lord shall give thee of this young woman."*
>
> **Verse 13:** *"The Lord gave her conception."*
>
> **Verse 14:** *"Blessed be the Lord, which hath not left thee this day without a kinsman."*

Very often, the Scriptures demonstrate that what is impossible with men is possible with God.

> **The birth of Isaac.** *"Is any thing too hard for the Lord?"* (Gen. 18:14).

**The birth of John the Baptist.** *"For with God nothing shall be impossible"* (Luke 1:37).

**The birth of the Lord.** *"This is the Lord's doing; it is marvellous in our eyes"* (Ps. 118:23).

## Serving

The name "Obed", that of the son of Boaz and Ruth, means "serving", reminding us that we have been saved to serve. The First Thessalonian epistle reminds us so much of the book of Ruth, and the two share some similarities. In every chapter of First Thessalonians we are told why they are saved. What marked the Thessalonians also marked Ruth;

**They turned to God from idols.** (1 Thess. 1:9) — The truth of Ruth 1.

**They served the living and true God.** (1 Thess. 1:9) — The truth of Ruth 2.

**They waited for his son from heaven.** (1 Thess. 1:10) — The truth of Ruth 3.

**They were delivered from coming wrath.** (1 Thess. 1:10) — The truth of Ruth 4.

In the context of "serving", it is important to notice how the men in that Thessalonian epistle are presented. They are seen as:

Evangelists
Examples
Fathers
Shepherds
Teachers
Nursing Mothers

## Four Practical Traits of Personalities in Chapter Four

The key positive personalities in the book of Ruth are Boaz, Ruth and Naomi, and from these three we can learn a lot to

# Ruth Fruitful in Marriage

apply in our own Christian lives. Lessons to be learned from Boaz, Ruth and Naomi form the basis of the outline here.

> **Boaz: The Redeemer**
> **Ruth: The One who Loves**
> **Ruth: The Builder**
> **Naomi: The Nurse**

## Boaz: The Redeemer

Boaz is both a **redeemer** and a **kinsman**.

### A Redeemer

Three things mark a true redeemer.

> He has **the right to redeem.**
> He has **the will to redeem.**
> He has **the power to redeem.**

We are Christ's by donation and Christ's by redemption.

> **We are Christ's by donation.** We are the love gift of the Father to the Son. *"Those whom thou hast given me"* (John 17:11).
>
> **We are Christ's by redemption.** Peter pointed out that we are elected by God, sanctified by the Spirit and born again by the Word of God. *"Being born again, not of corruptible seed, but of incorruptible, by the word of God, which liveth and abideth forever"* (1 Pet. 1:23).

We are redeemed by precious blood. Now, the most corruptible thing you and I know is blood, and among the most incorruptible things we know of are silver and gold. But Peter says, *"Ye were not redeemed with corruptible things, as silver and gold...but with the precious blood of Christ, as of a lamb without blemish and without spot"* (1 Pet. 1:18-19).

> Redeemed how I love to proclaim it!
> Redeemed by the blood of the Lamb.

# GLEANINGS FROM THE BOOK OF RUTH

Redeemed through His infinite mercy,
His child, and for ever, I am.

*Redeemed*, Fanny Crosby

Boaz, the redeemer, became the father of Obed, in whom we see **progress**. Obed is seen as;

**A babe:** *"For thy daughter-in-law...hath borne him"* (v. 15).

**A child:** *"And Naomi took the child...and became nurse unto it"* (v. 16).

**A son:** *"And the women her neighbours gave it a name, saying, There is a son born to Naomi, and they called his name Obed"* (v. 17).

**A father:** *"Obed: he is the father of Jesse, the father of David"* (v. 17).

While the sonship of Obed is special, the Sonship of Christ is unique, which is why He could say, *"I ascend unto my Father, and your Father"* (John 20:17). He knew the Father in a way that you and I don't know Him.

As the **Son of Abraham** He is heir to the land.

As the **Son of David** He is heir to the throne.

As the **Son of Man** He is heir to the world.

As the **Son of God** He is heir of all things.

### *The "Nearer Kinsman"*

There are two words for kinsman in the book of Ruth. One word simply means an acquaintance, or a relative. The other is a person, usually a near relative, who is in a position to buy or purchase that which has been lost, usually in connection with the family inheritance. This is seen in the person of Boaz, the one who was willing to redeem as well as able to redeem, in comparison to the nearer kinsman, who was willing to redeem the land but was not willing to redeem the person.

Who does the "nearer kinsman" represent? There are three-possibilities of the picture represented by this man, who was willing but not able.

## Ruth Fruitful in Marriage

**A brother.** Some have supposed that there was a brother of Elimelech, who therefore would be a nearer kinsman than Boaz.

**Human effort.** Others have suggested that the nearer kinsman can be likened to works for justification. They think they can pay for salvation, although the price has been paid already.

> Jesus paid it all,
> All to Him I owe.
> Sin had left a crimson stain,
> He washed it white as snow.
>
> *Jesus Paid it All*, Elvina M. Hall

The work is all done, for, on the cross, the Lord said, *"It is finished"* (John 19:30). The principle is further clarified in the Psalms, *"They that trust in their wealth, and boast themselves in the multitude of their riches; None of them can by any means redeem his brother, nor give to God a ransom for him"* (Ps. 49:6-7).

**The Law.** To my mind, the near kinsman would represent the law, of which there was nothing wrong in itself. The law is holy, perfect, just and good. The problem was that the flesh had to keep the law in order for the law to redeem, and the flesh is too weak and cannot do that.

For us today, the equivalent is presented by Paul, when he wrote, *"When the fullness of the time was come, God sent forth his Son, made of a woman, made under the law, To redeem them that were under the law, that we might receive the adoption of sons"* (Gal. 4:4-5). *"For what the law could not do, in that it was weak through the flesh (... God did)"* (Romans 8:3).

In the 4$^{th}$ chapter of Ruth, the picture is straightforward. The near kinsman, like the law, is willing (he said, *"I will redeem it"*, v. 4) but is not able (he said to Boaz, *"I cannot redeem it for myself... redeem thou my right to thyself; for I cannot redeem it"* (v. 6).

# GLEANINGS FROM THE BOOK OF RUTH

Ruth: The One Who Loves

You cannot read through the book of Ruth and not be impressed that here is a woman marked by love.

> **She loves God.**
>
> **She loves the people of God.** *"Thy people shall be my people, and thy God my God"* (1:16).
>
> **She loves Boaz.**
>
> **She loves the field** belonging to Boaz.
>
> **She loves Naomi** her mother-in-law.

### David *as an example of Love*

It is a characteristic of the last days that people go wrong in their affections. They are lovers of self, lovers of silver, lovers of that which is not good and lovers of pleasures rather than lovers of God. I like to read the Psalms, and especially to read about David's love.

> **David loved the people of God.** *"But to the saints that are in the earth, and to the excellent, in whom is all my delight"* (Ps. 16:3).
>
> **David loved the House of God.** *"Lord, I have loved the habitation of thy house, and the place where thine honour dwelleth"* (Ps. 26:8).
>
> If you have the *"I love"* of Psalm 26, you will have the *"I desire"* of Psalm 27. *"One thing have I desired of the Lord, that will I seek after; that I may dwell in the house of the Lord all the days of my life"* (Ps. 27:4).
>
> **David loved the Lord.** *"I love the Lord, because he hath heard my voice and supplications"* (Ps. 116:1).
>
> **David loved the Word of God.** *"I will delight myself in thy commandments, which I have loved"* (Ps. 119:47).

# Ruth Fruitful in Marriage

## *Love of the Assembly*

Just as David loved the house of God in his day, we ought to love the assembly of God in our day. If you love the assembly of God there are four things you will not do. You will not:

> **Desert it.** That means you will not miss any meetings; worship meetings, prayer meetings, Bible study meetings or gospel meetings.
>
> **Despise it.** *"What? Have ye not houses to eat and to drink in? or despise ye the church of God?"* (1 Cor. 11:22).
>
> **Defile it.** *"If any man defile the temple of God, him shall God destroy; for the temple of God is holy, which temple ye are"* (1 Cor. 3:17).
>
> **Divide it.** *"Mark them which cause divisions and offenses contrary to the doctrine which ye have learned; and avoid them"* (Rom. 16:17).

You will pray for its **peace**, for its **purity**, for its **preservation** and its **perfection**.

## Ruth: The Builder

The thought of a "builder" is common throughout the Word of God, and Ruth is an example of this, in that her desire is to build up the inheritance of the people of God, as it should be ours. *"But ye, beloved, building up yourselves on your most holy faith"* (Jude 20). It is important that we build up ourselves before we seek to abound unto the edifying and building up of the church.

Applying the same thoughts to the New Testament, believers are seen as **worshippers, witnesses, comforters** and **builders**.

### *Every Christian Ought to Be a Worshipper*

*"We are the circumcision, which worship God in the Spirit"* (Phil. 3:3).

> **There will come a time when we will not need the evangelist.** Today we need those who preach the gospel, but only for a time.

# GLEANINGS FROM THE BOOK OF RUTH

> God's house is filling fast
> Yet there is room!
> Some soul will be the last,
> Yet there is room!

**There will come a time when we will not need the teacher.** Today we need him for correction, and counsel and comfort. We won't need him in glory.

**There will come a time when we will not need the shepherd.** Today we need him to care for the flock. The time will come when we will not need him.

**But there will never come a time when we will not need the worshipper.**

One of the things we are going to do in heaven we are going to worship the Lamb.

> But still as we study Him more,
> And ponder His works and His ways,
> New beauties unnoticed before
> Are blossoming out to our gaze.

### *Every Christian Ought to Be a Witness Bearer*

"*Ye also shall bear witness, because ye have been with me from the beginning*" (John 15:27).

### *Every Christian Ought to Be a Comforter*

God does not comfort us to make us comfortable, but rather to make us comforters. We have to comfort others where we ourselves have been comforted of God (2 Cor. 1:4).

### *Every Christian ought to Be a Builder.*

"*Seek that ye may excel* (abound) *to the edifying of the church*" (1 Cor. 14:12).

## Naomi: The Nurse

So the book ends with a child in a nurse's arms. Little is said about the child and no details are recorded about the nurse

## Ruth Fruitful in Marriage

(beyond what we knew already) but the principle of care is established, and the story ends with a link to the royal tree and all that that entailed. A nurse, in a figurative sense, is one who feeds and protects, or gives aid and comfort, and the thought of a nurse is most prevalent, not just in the church age, but in previous dispensations.

So Naomi is an illustration of a greater truth—the role of a nursing character in biblical times—and brings in important truths of **care and communion**. We should spend time **with** Christ as well as spend time **for** Him.

The Lord Jesus chose 12—that they might be with Him and that He might send them forth to preach. He had a private life with God as well as a public life for God. There is a danger of being occupied for Christ at the expense of being occupied with Him.

We see many examples of **care and communion** in the Scriptures.

**Christ in the bosom of the Father** (John 1:18). This is the place of communion. Christ is ever and always in the Father's bosom. It is He who knows the Father's bosom as His dwelling place. He, and He alone, could say, *"I knew that thou hearest me always"* (John 11:42).

> Morning by morning Thou didst wake,
> Amidst this poisoned air;
> Yet no contagion touched Thy soul,
> No sin disturbed Thy prayer.
>
> *A Perfect Path of Purest Grace,* Wylie MacLeod

**The disciple whom Jesus loved reclining (leaning) on Jesus' bosom** (John 13:23). The place of **closeness**.

**Lazarus in the bosom of Abraham** (Luke 16:23). The place of **comfort**. Now he is comforted and thou art tormented.

**The lamb in the bosom of the shepherd** (Isaiah 40:11). The place of being **carried**.

**The child in the bosom of Naomi** (Ruth 4:16). The place of **care**.

Spiritually, this is similar to the work of the shepherd in the church age. Paul is a good example of a spiritual nurse, and he talks of:

**Travailing in birth.** *"My little children, of whom I travail in birth again until Christ be formed in you"* (Gal. 4:19).

**Cherishing.** *"But we were gentle among you, even as a nurse cherisheth her children"* (1 Thess. 2:7).

# THE "UNTILS" OF THE BOOK OF RUTH

The book of Ruth, in common with so many other books in the Scriptures, contains themes that allow for enlargement. One of these is represented by the word "until". The word is mentioned nine times in the book, and from these we can glean lessons that go beyond the immediate scope of the short story. In particular, four prominent "untils" stand out, and these are developed here as examples of gleanings to be derived from such specific cases:

### The "Until" of Companionship
*"So they two went until they came to Bethlehem* (Judah)*"* (1:19).

### The "Until" of Continuance
*"*(She) *hath continued even from the morning until now"* (2:7).

### The "Until" of Communion
*"And she lay at his feet until the morning"* (3:14).

### The "Until" of Completion
*"The man will not be in rest, until he have finished the thing this day"* (3:18).

## The "Until" of Companionship

*"So they two went until they came to Bethlehem* (Judah)*"* (1:19).

Naomi and Ruth travelled the road together, illustrating the principle of companionship being a **walk together,** both physically and spiritually. From this journey of **recovery** back to an inheritance, we consider the walk together for those of like mind, the recovery from backsliding and the arrival at a new **home**. Also, there is the **pattern** that Ruth chose to follow

Naomi as opposed to Orpah—and the blessings enjoyed as suggested by the use of the word *"more"* (v. 17).

## Going Together

The picture of Naomi and Ruth travelling together on the same path and being of one mind is reflected in other Scriptures, and in the Godhead too.

> **A mother-in-law and a daughter-in-law.** *"So they two went until they came to Bethlehem* (Judah)*"* (1:19). Until they came to Bethlehem - the house of bread. Failure with God is never final. In that regard the use of the word *"again"* by Naomi is very important. In verse 21 she says, *"the Lord hath brought me home again"*, reminding us how patient and how longsuffering God is with us. In the same way God was longsuffering with Jonah after his initial disobedience, for we read that the *"word of the Lord came unto Jonah the second time"* (Jon. 3:1).
>
> **A master and a servant.** In 2 Kings chapter 2 Elijah and Elisha went on together to Bethel, to Jericho, and to Jordan. In this we can see the continuation of the testimony, a pattern that is repeated with others. We read that:
>
>> Moses goes out and Joshua goes on,
>> Eli goes out and Samuel goes on,
>> David goes out and Solomon goes on,
>> Paul goes out and Timothy goes on.
>> In this case, Elijah goes out and Elisha goes on.
>
> **A father and a son.** In Genesis chapter 22 Abraham the father and Isaac the son went both together to the place of sacrifice, showing a oneness, a unity and a togetherness.

This oneness between a father and a son reminds us of the closeness of the Father and the Son, specifically as recorded in John's gospel.

> **The love the Father has for the Son.** *"The Father loveth the Son, and hath given all things into his hand"* (John 3:35).

## The "Untils" of the Book of Ruth

*"The Father loveth the Son, and sheweth him all things that himself doeth"* (John 5:20).

**The Son's love for the Father.** *"That the world may know that I love the Father;...Arise, let us go hence"* (John 14:31).

The Father loves the Son who ever pleased Him well
Each movement of that Holy One some beauty forth doth tell.

### Recovery

The picture of Naomi (with Ruth) travelling back to the land she should not have left, makes Ruth chapter 1 a chapter of backsliding and recovery. Briefly (for this has been covered in Section C), when a person backslides they depart from a **place**, a **people** and a **person**. This is what Elimelech and Naomi, and Mahlon and Chilion did.

Thus, when a person is recovered they return to a **place**, a **people** and a **person**. This is what Naomi did, and leads us to consider this and other recoveries in Scripture.

> **The recovery of Naomi.** *"I went out full, and the Lord hath brought me home again empty"* (1:21).
>
> **The recovery of a brother.** Abraham *"brought back all the goods, and also brought again his brother Lot"* (Gen. 14:16).
>
> **The recovery of a nazarite** as seen in Samson. *"The hair of his head began to grow again"* (Judg. 16:22).
>
> **The recovery of a king.** *"Jehoshaphat dwelt at Jerusalem: and he went out again through* (among) *the people"* (2 Chron. 19:4).

### Home

For Naomi, Bethlehem-Judah was home. When she was recovered, she **came home**, but acknowledges it was the Lord who **brought her home**. Home, relative to one's condition, can be viewed in a threefold way in the Scriptures.

**Go home.** The Lord said this to the man who had had his dwellings among the tombs. *"Go home to thy friends, and tell them how great things the Lord has done for thee"* (Mark 5:19).

**At home.** We are told we shall be absent from the body and at home with the Lord (2 Cor. 5:8).

**Brought home.** Naomi said, *"I went out full, and the Lord hath brought me home again empty"* (1:21). That lesson for us today is that we should never forget the death of Christ, and never forget the cross of Christ. The death of Christ fits me for heaven, and the cross of Christ finishes me for earth.

## Pattern

To a greater or lesser extent, we are influenced in life by the example set by others and much depends on the pattern we choose to follow. For Ruth, Naomi is the pattern, and this is evident on the road to her "new" home, when she is tested in a threefold way:

The **pull** for home.

The **perplexities** of life.

The **pattern** of others.

The result of this testing is that Ruth clave to Naomi. Essentially, Ruth says, "Orpah is not the pattern of my life. You, Naomi, are the pattern of my life." The only thing that will part them is death. Notice, in chapter 1:16-17, the choices she makes:

**Her path.** *"Whither thou goest, I will go"* (v. 16). The path that your feet move in, my feet will move in.

**Her dwelling place.** *"Where thou lodgest, I will lodge"* (v. 16). Where you stay, I will stay.

**Her people.** *"Thy people shall be my people"* (v. 16). The people you company with and fellowship with, I will fellowship with as well.

**Her God.** *"Thy God my God"* (v. 16). The God you worship and the God you serve, I will worship and I will serve.

## The "Untils" of the Book of Ruth

**Her death.** *"Where thou diest, will I die...the Lord do so to me, and more also, if ought but death part thee and me"* (v. 17). I will be buried where you are.

## "More"

Think on the little word *"more"*, as used by Boaz to describe Ruth. It brings before us the thought of growth and advancement, not only here, but in other Scriptures too.

**More kindness.** Ruth *"shewed more kindness in the latter end than at the beginning, inasmuch as thou followedst not young men, whether poor or rich"* (3:10).

**More growth.** Isaac *"waxed great, and went forward"* (Gen. 26:13). Or—he grew more.

**More behaviour.** *"David behaved himself more wisely than all the servants of Saul"* (1 Sam. 18:30).

**More fruit & much fruit.** In John 15 we see fruit; *"more fruit"* in verse 2, and *"much fruit"* in verse 5.

**More strength.** It says about Saul that he *"increased the more in strength"* (Acts 9:22).

## The "Until" of Continuance

*"(She) hath continued even from the morning until now"* (2:7).

Ruth is known for what we would call "her stickability". Her attitude to gleaning, when she goes on steadily for a long time, is noticed by the servant and commended by Boaz. This example leads us to a consideration of the importance of going on **continually**, and with **consistency**. The latter is illustrated here by a consideration of the attitude of believers in the early days of the church age.

### Continually

There are certain things we have to do continually.

We have **continually to seek God**. *"Seek the Lord and his strength, seek his face continually"* (1 Chron. 16:11).

We have **continually to offer the sacrifice of praise** to God. *"Let us offer the sacrifice of praise to God continually"* (Heb. 13:15).

We have **continually to serve God.** It was said to Daniel, *"Thy God whom thou servest continually"* (Dan. 6:16).

Consistency

In reading through the Acts of the Apostles it is evident that consistency marked the early church. This shows in attitudes to worship, teaching and the gospel.

> **With one accord.** *"These all continued with one accord in prayer and supplication, with the women"* (Acts 1:14).
>
> **Stedfastly.** *"They continued stedfastly in the apostles' doctrine and fellowship, and in breaking of bread, and in prayers"* (Acts 2:42).
>
> **Continually.** *"They ceased not to teach and preach Jesus Christ"* (Acts 5:42).

Have you ever noticed in the Acts of the Apostles how prayer is not only continual, but prominent and preeminent?

> **Prayer before ministry.** *"We will give ourselves continually to prayer, and to the ministry of the word* (Acts 6:4).
>
> **Prayer before preaching.** *"Behold, he prayeth"* (Acts 9:11). Then we see Paul preaching verse 20.
>
> **Prayer before praise.** *"Paul and Silas prayed, and sang praises unto God: and the prisoners heard them"* (Acts 16:25).

## The "Until" Of Communion.

*"And she lay at his feet until the morning"* (3:14).

The idea of being "at the feet" is that of communion, of one-mindedness. Ruth lies at Boaz's feet until the morning. It is significant that she gets more at the feet than she does in the field.

Whereas in the field she gets handfuls, at the feet she gets lapfuls.

# The "Untils" of the Book of Ruth

The principle of "being at the feet", and thus being in communion, is exemplified by others at the feet of Christ. We show this from a number of scenes taken from Luke's gospel, and go on to consider the record of Mary before reflecting on the outcome of communion.

## Others at the Feet of Christ

In Luke's gospel we read about the feet of Christ. Some are standing at the feet of Christ, and others are lying, falling or sitting.

> **Standing.** The woman in Luke chapter 7 is standing at the feet of Christ. She is **washing,** she is **weeping,** she is **wiping,** and she is **worshipping** while standing at the feet of Christ.
>
> **Lying.** Jairus in Luke chapter 8 is lying at the feet of Jesus. He is beseeching Him to come to his house.
>
> **Falling.** The Samaritan in Luke chapter 17 returns and falls at the feet of Christ, and thanks Him. The only one out of the ten. Nine are taken up with their blessings, but the one is taken up with the Blesser.
>
> **Sitting.** The man in Luke chapter 8, who had the demons cast out from him, is sitting, clothed and in his right mind. He prayed that he might be with Him.

## Example of Mary

Mary is a woman who communes at the feet of Christ (see comments earlier in Section E).

> In Luke chapter 10 she is **sitting at His feet.** Mary is listening.
>
> In John chapter 11 she **falls at His feet.** Mary is weeping.
>
> In John chapter 12 she is **standing at His feet.** Mary is anointing and wiping.

Mary is criticised while at His feet communing, by Martha, by the disciples and by Judas. (See comments in Section E).

# GLEANINGS FROM THE BOOK OF RUTH

But what is the important thing in life? It's not what we think of ourselves, nor what others think of us. It's what God thinks of us. What else matters if God approves? Jesus of Nazareth, we read, was a man approved of God by miracles, wonders and signs. God commends Mary, saying she has chosen that good part. While the disciples say, "why this waste", the Lord says *"she hath wrought a good work"* (Mark 14:6).

## Outcome of Communion

The book of Ruth highlights communion and illustrates its importance in a believer's life, for we become like the company we keep. Our company either makes us or mars us. *"He that walketh with wise men shall be wise: but a companion of fools shall be destroyed"* (Prov. 13:20). Ruth is characterised by communion with Naomi and the outcome of that is a linking of kindred spirits for the good of each. The effects of communion are exemplified in the Scriptures by what it does to our appearance, our courage and our works, and leads to a consideration of some aspects of Christ's appearance.

**Communion made Moses' face to shine.** The skin of his face shone by reason of him speaking with Him. Moses was not aware of it and was not going through the camp saying, "Look at my face, it's shining". *"Moses wist* (knew) *not that the skin of his face shone"* (Ex. 34:29).

> Oh for the shining of the face.
> Oh for the ignorance of the shining.

**Communion produces boldness.** *"When they saw the boldness of Peter and John, and perceived that they were unlearned and ignorant men ..... they took knowledge of them, that they had been with Jesus"* (Acts 4:13).

**Communion produces fruit.** *"The branch cannot bear fruit of itself, except it abide in the vine; no more can ye, except ye abide in me"* (John 15:4).

> Happy if in God confiding,
> Fruitful if in Christ abiding,

## The "Untils" of the Book of Ruth

> Holy through the Spirit guiding.
> Peace is mine.

Since the presence of God affected Moses' outward appearance, so Christ's outward appearance is worthy of our attention. We read of the face, the form, the features and the feet of Christ:

**The face of Christ.** *"His visage was so marred more than any man, and his form more than the sons of men"* (Isa. 52:14).

**The form of Christ.** *"Who, being in the form of God…took upon him the form of a servant"* (Phil. 2:6-7).

> The form of God to Him pertained complete equality.
> Was not an object to be gained for very God was He.

**The features of Christ.** Meekness and gentleness characterised Christ. *"I am meek and lowly in heart"* (Matt. 11:29). *"…by the meekness and gentleness of Christ"* (2 Cor. 10:1).

> In every feature flawless,
> In every aspect fair
> The search of sinners lawless,
> Could find no blemish there.

**The Feet of Christ.** His feet never strayed, never stumbled, never slipped and never did slide. His were feet that were beautiful. *"How beautiful upon the mountains are the feet of him that bringeth good tidings, that publisheth peace"* (Isa. 52:7).

> We thank thee oh His Father God for Thy beloved Son.
> For all the way His feet have trod and all His hands have done.

What is produced by being at the feet of Christ is seen in gratitude, in praise, in worship and in thanksgiving.

> What matters else since God approves,
> None can distract, none can deter.
> Obediently he onward moves,
> The cross to reach and triumph there.

# GLEANINGS FROM THE BOOK OF RUTH

## The "Until" of Completion.

*"The man will not be in rest, until he have finished the thing this day"* (3:18).

In the story of Naomi, Ruth and Boaz no loose ends are left hanging, for all is wound up and completed, ending with the royal line being preserved. This example is followed elsewhere, as reflected in the book of Philippians.

> **A work commenced.** *"He which hath begun a good work in you will perform it until the day of Jesus Christ"* (Phil. 1:6).
>
> **A work continued.** *"It is God which worketh in you both to will and to do of his good pleasure"* (Phil. 2:13).
>
> **A work completed.** He is going to *"change our vile body, that it may be fashioned like unto his glorious body"* (Phil. 3:21). Our redemption is not complete. As to the soul it is complete.

> O perfect redemption, the purchase of blood;
> To every believer the free gift of God;
> The vilest offender who truly believes
> That moment, through Jesus, a pardon receives.
>
> *To God be the Glory*, Fanny Crosby

But as to the body it is not complete. We wait the redemption of the body.

> Long as my life shall last,
> Teach me thy way!
> Where'er my lot is cast,
> Teach me thy way!
> Until the race is run,
> Until the journey's done,
> Until the crown is won,
> Teach me thy way.
>
> *Teach Me Thy Way, O Lord*, Benjamin M. Ramsey